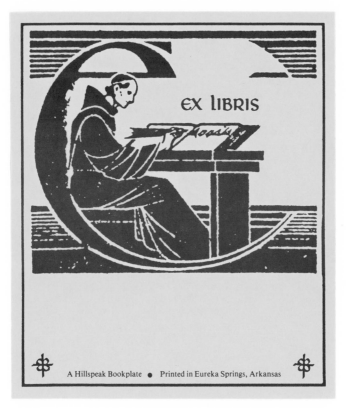

EX LIBRIS

A Hillspeak Bookplate ● Printed in Eureka Springs, Arkansas

The Word Is Very Near You

"*The word is very near you;*
it is in your mouth and in your heart,
so that you can do it."
—*Deuteronomy* 30:14

Also by Martin L. Smith

Reconciliation:
Preparing for Confession in
the Episcopal Church

THE · WORD · IS VERY · NEAR YOU

A GUIDE TO PRAYING WITH SCRIPTURE

MARTIN L. SMITH

1989

COWLEY PUBLICATIONS

Cambridge, Massachusetts

Published in the United States of America by Cowley Publications, a
division of the Society of St. John the Evangelist. All rights reserved.
No portion of this book may be reproduced in whole or in part
without the consent of Cowley Publications except in the case of
brief quotations embodied in critical articles and reviews.

International Standard Book Number:
0-936384-97-2, cloth
0-936384-81-6, paper
Library of Congress Number:
89-22144

Cover Illustration and Design by Daniel Earl Thaxton
Book Design by Daniel Earl Thaxton

Library of Congress Cataloging-in-Publications Data
Smith, Martin Lee.
    The word is very near you : a guide to praying with Scrip-
ture / Martin L. Smith.
      p.   cm.
    ISBN 0-936384-97-2 : $16.95 cloth
          0-936384-81-6 : $9.95 paper
    1. Prayer.   I. Title.   II. Title: Praying with Scripture.
BV215.S63
248.3'2—dc20   89-22144

This book is printed on acid-free paper and produced in
the United States of America

Cowley Publications
980 Memorial Drive
Cambridge, Massachusetts 02138

*For my brothers
in the Society of St. John the Evangelist
in thankfulness for our life together
and the reality of the love
which we share.*

Contents

Preface

In my work of teaching prayer and giving spiritual direction, many people have asked me to suggest a book which they could use to learn ways of praying with Scripture. I longed to recommend a book which would satisfy this need for practical teaching while meeting further conditions. First, there are thousands of people serious about prayer whose knowledge of contemporary biblical criticism is enough to make them allergic to the simplistic, semi-fundamentalist vein in which so many "spiritual" books about Scripture are written. So the book must show that the meditative use of Scripture is compatible with well-grounded interpretation of the Bible. Second, many of these seekers do not have an adequate familiarity with the Bible to find easily passages to pray with. So the book must help them in the early stages of learning to meditate by suggesting hundreds of places in Scripture to turn to. Third, I have found that people cannot take in teaching about ways to pray unless deeper questions are tackled first. So the book needed to raise questions about who God is, and what it is about us that makes intimacy between God and human beings possible, and not only possible but the very thing we most need and seek, and yet avoid.

I could not find the book I wanted to recommend so I decided to create it.

In Part 1 I invite the readers to examine their presuppositions about prayer and discover an approach in which we are primarily receptive. I explore the human need for relationship and how the God who is Father, Son and Holy Spirit encounters us at every level of that need. Then I show how meditative prayer with Scripture opens us to that three-fold encounter and intimacy.

After exploring the various ways God uses Scripture to communicate, there follows teaching about the practice of meditative prayer and its place in the rhythms of our daily lives. Three ways of praying with Scripture are taught: meditation with stories, "holy reading," in which we meditate with single words or phrases which have arisen from our slow, receptive reading of passages, and contemplative prayer with images from Scripture.

Part 2 consists of series of Scripture citations clustered around a variety of themes. Each biblical reference is accompanied by a short title or quotation to identify the main thrust of the passage, and a caption which suggests one of the many ways we could pray with it. The clusters can be used in various ways. Readers can easily select one or two passages from those listed, or they can explore a theme over time, taking each passage in turn.

Psalm quotations are from the Book of Common Prayer of the Episcopal Church, and all other Scripture quotations are from the Revised Standard Version.

The book has been written for use not only by individuals, but as a resource for groups who meet to foster the life of prayer. The accounts of religious experience found here have been fictionalized in order to protect confidentiality.

Martin L. Smith SSJE
Cambridge, Mass.

PART I

1

Pausing At The Threshold

Why have you picked up this book about prayer? I wish I had the courage to insist that this book begin with a good number of blank pages which you could fill with your answer to that question. There is a precedent. When Charles Péguy published his first long poem on Joan of Arc he left some pages blank, as he said, "To give you time to think."

Why do you want to read a book about prayer? Why now? What kind of readiness and receptivity do you have? What do you desire? What are you looking for?

The time used in uncovering the answers to these questions could be well spent. Think what kind of book this appears to be. It sets out to communicate some of the arts of meditative prayer using Scripture and it offers directions for beginners to find paths of prayer through what is for many the strange country of the Bible. It looks like a definitely practical book. It clearly aims to teach and guide. Yet the goal lies beyond technique and method. The aim is to foster intimacy with God, no less. (Intimacy! With God! What would *that* involve?) Can a *book* really help here? Can it fulfill such a promise?

Books claiming power, radiant with promises, are everywhere. "How-to" books and "self-help" books, books which promise to turn our lives around by means of the techniques and insights which they describe, range over almost every conceivable aspect of life. The claim to power is itself powerful and such books are commercially successful. They appeal to our unconscious religiosity; we are susceptible, sometimes pathetically so, to promises of salvation. Something deep within us vibrates in response to images of success and serenity, of manageable relationships and loves that work, of coherent feelings, desirable skills, bodily well-being and psychic strength. A book which is laden with the freight of images of fulfillment can exercise an almost talismanic power. Buying one at the airport bookstand is a transaction that can have an almost mythic dimension. We act out of unconscious desire for magical empowerment by means of an object, in this case not a lamp or jewel, but a text, the oracles of a hero or prophetess, spells to bring about our transformation. The disappointment we experience with most of these books is a clue to the unconscious forces that were at work when our interest was aroused. Disillusioned again, we realize that transformation is not to be had on the cheap. The answers to our problems cannot be bought off the shelf after all. Our expectations were unrealistic.

Perhaps too our hearts had their defenses well in place to resist the possibilities of change. Sometimes our enthusiasm masks a cynical defensiveness about books that promise change in our lives. Often their prescriptions of self-discipline and suggestions of new ways of understanding life are rational, of proven value, and lie within the range of our capabilities yet we often only toy with their recommendations in a desultory way. We lack the motivation to change,

Pausing At The Threshold

we even fear it, and our cooperation with the wisdom of a writer is sabotaged by unconscious resistance. We lose interest in the book or reject it, blaming the writer for being too simplistic, perhaps.

If you take notice of your feelings as you begin this book, don't be surprised at finding them to be ambivalent. You are probably attracted *and* somewhat mistrustful. On the one hand, there is something fascinating about the prospect of a rich life of prayer even when we cannot begin to imagine what that would be like. Perhaps you feel stirred by a sense that prayer could really take on a new depth and intensity and the book feels like the clue to the beginning of an adventure. On the other hand, your attitude may be quite guarded at the same time. Is there an inner voice trying to warn you that this may be no more than another of those "how-to-pray" books that come out all the time? Some of them encourage us for a while when we are in the mood for spirituality but we quickly lose patience with them. At best we dip into them on the lookout for helpful hints, rather than for a radical development of our praying. Finally we relegate them to a bookshelf, as we might do with yet another cookbook that did not stay in the kitchen long.

I suggest you smile at these feelings if you recognize them within yourself. The drama of attraction and mistrust is played out in almost everything we do; there is a lot of comedy in it. It is good to admit our muddle and ambivalence into consciousness and give our humanness recognition salted with humor. It would be surprising if we were not susceptible both to the mirage of "success" in prayer, and to the inertia of resistance. We are human.

But what else is going on as you take up a book about prayer? Perhaps you actually desire God. Perhaps the true origin of the straightforward act of opening this book on prayer is attraction to God. Perhaps beneath the surface reactions of enthusiasm or skepticism there is a simple motive that has great dignity, a flame of desire that ought to be respected and cherished. Many of us have never received any encouragement to recognize or honor within ourselves the desire for God. The expression seems too sublime to be applied to the faint movements of our own spirit. To speak to most others about having a desire for God would cause embarrassment and even invite ridicule. No one talks like this in "normal" life. But it is not merely to protect ourselves from the patronizing skepticism of others that we tend to cover up spiritual yearning. Most of us have an inner voice which is cynical about the reality of our own religious experience. In a secular climate we have become our own oppressors, adept at disparaging and discounting the movements of our own hearts. One of the results of praying is a gradual healing of these patterns of self-devaluation, and liberation from those inhibitions that cripple our capacity to honor ourselves as men and women of God. You may be only in the very early stages of this healing, but right now it is possible to begin to break the habit of pinching off the buds of new life within yourself.

You are beginning a book about prayer. It may be the first or the fiftieth you have read. You may be literally a beginner or you may be beginning again, as most of us have to do many times over in our life with God. Begin by honoring the desire

Pausing At The Threshold

9

that is in you for God. To want to pray is to want God. That is a wonderful thing. The flame may be weak and flickering; all the more reason for cupping hands of trust around it.

When we have realized that our motive for learning more about prayer (even though it suffers distortion and drag from our common woundedness and inertia) springs from an inner source of true desire for God that is worthy of deep respect, we might feel ready to go forward. Is there any further reason for lingering on the threshold? There is another question to ask. Where does your desire for prayer—for God—come *from?*

We have already been answering the question at one level. When we come to self-awareness about why we are exploring prayer we find ourselves using the language of depth and inwardness to do justice to our attraction. "Deep down," we find ourselves saying, "I want to get to know God." Scripture provides us with an array of traditional images for the inner core where our most important desires spring up, most prominently the heart.

But does the desire for God originate within ourselves as a spontaneous reaching out of the human spirit? A breakthrough of faith occurs when we recognize that our desire for God originates not in ourselves but in God. It is God who gives, kindles and fuels the desire for God. What we feel as our desire is the effect of God desiring to be desired, knowing that our responsive desiring will bring us to life. Those who give themselves entirely to the response to God, whom we call mystics, come back from their explorations and tell us that they discover in the end that our desiring is all God's doing. We love with God's own loving that flows from God, gathers us up in its movement, and returns to God, bearing us along! Of course as beginners we don't know that yet. But since in the community of Christ we are learning to depend on one another to make sense of life and the spiritual journey, we can accept this ultimate discovery in faith and take it to heart as just what we need to hear now as beginners. This in fact will be our starting point in the next chapter. Now as you pause on the threshold asking yourself why you have been moved to read a book on prayer, and why just now, you can allow your faith to trace the answer right back to God. God's initiative is at work here, grace is active drawing and inviting you to deeper intimacy with God. Trust the truth of this. It means respecting and cherishing this impulse to investigate prayer all the more. As a desire coming from deep within yourself, it is wonderful. As a gift and stirring of God, it is holy.

As you ask yourself where the desire to read a book about prayer is coming from, it may occur to you to wonder where the desire to write it came from! As I have mentioned in the preface there are straightforward practical reasons for writing this book. Again and again in trying to initiate men and women into the practice of meditating with Scripture I have found myself wanting to be able to put into their hands a book that would give them the help they were asking for, and to make it available to those who had no opportunity to receive personal coaching in prayer. Rather than wait for someone else to produce just what was called for, I set about creating it myself. There was a straightforward challenge to my creativity. In addition to this creative urge, there is a desire to share some of what I have received from others.

From an early age I have known hundreds of women and men of God and had access to their wisdom about prayer in conversations, retreats, talks and writings. There is an organic process always at work in the church, called tradition, in which the living experience of God is transmitted from generation to generation and from person to person. Much of my own personal experience is reflected in these pages, but little of the teaching is original in the usual sense of the word. Rather, as you read the pages, you are being touched by the experience of hundreds of men and women of prayer in many different parts of the world from whom I have learnt and am still learning so much. However, these answers in terms of the urge to create and share are not entirely adequate. For who is the ground and source of this creativity in writing? Who inspires the sharing by which we meet one another's needs?

Here too God has the initiative. God is continually working to create and revive the means of drawing us all into intimacy. If a book about prayer may be instrumental in helping just a few hundred seekers further into that intimacy, then God rejoices to help bring it to life and through providence bring it into the hands of those who could be nourished by it. Writing it becomes an act of prayer in response to God's stimulus and attraction. One of the signs of God's initiative is that writing this book has become a continuous act of intercession, as I find myself praying intently for those who will read it. I find myself experiencing the desire in prayer which Pascal once expressed: "If this discourse pleases you and seems impressive, know that it is made by a man who has knelt, both before and after it, in prayer to that Being, infinite and without parts, before whom he lays all he has, for you also to lay before Him all you have for your own good and His glory so that strength may be given to lowliness."

As you become aware of your feelings at the beginning of this book maybe you sense a need to know that you are not alone in your desire to pray and your desire for God. Prayer always draw us into relationship with those others who are also exploring the mystery. You are not alone. You are in my prayers and those of many others, as you open the book. Prayer and the desire for prayer draws us out of isolation into the greatest of communities, the ultimate one, the communion of saints.

Pausing At The Threshold

2

God Is A Conversation

Prayer is a conversation with God. This is how most people would define prayer. What they would mean is a conversation that *we are expected to begin*. Prayer is saying something to God and receiving an answer, we would confidently assert. But our confidence in the standard definition often masks all sorts of misgivings and confusions about what kind of conversation this is.

First, what kind of answers do we in fact hear in response to our prayer? What do I expect from God's side of the conversation? Some of us have, by trial and error mainly, come to regard certain welcome feelings of consolation and encouragement, certain illuminating ideas or suggestive words of Scripture coming to mind, or certain kinds of inner urgings that rise up after we have spoken, as the ways in which God is "answering" us. But in the experience of many of us, these kinds of answers are fewer and farther between than seems to be implied by the notion of conversation. Why is God's side of the conversation, if this is what those inspirations and urgings are, so sparse and sporadic? Very faithful Christians praying along these lines can find that more often than not, listening for such answers is just a strained silence repeatedly broken by the "static" of our random thoughts.

Preachers have the habit of urging us to listen for God's voice, but we seldom get any guidance about what this listening is supposed to consist in. We assume it means "treading water," with the flotsam and jetsam of our wandering thoughts flowing around us in eddies, while we wait for inspiration or a guiding idea. Since this requires a lot of endurance and proves to be so often fruitless, there is a natural tendency to fall back on the idea that God "answers" prayer not so much by communicating with us in the prayer time but by performing some later action for us in response to a request of ours. Many people do not expect to "hear" God in prayer. For them an answer to prayer is a subsequent event, something we asked to happen in a certain way, such as the recovery of a friend from illness. They look for answers to prayer in the way things turn out, trying to find what is capable of being interpreted as a favor or refusal from God. God's side of the conversation of prayer tends to be regarded as a rather laconic affair of yes or no, wait or maybe, conveyed through the sign-language of events and non-events.

If you recognize yourself, however faintly, in the mirror of this description it could be the occasion of a most valuable insight. No wonder if your experience of prayer was mostly uphill and that you have been subject to discouragement and the feeling of disappointment that you can get "so far and no further" in prayer. Perhaps your frustration is a most important indicator that something basic has been wrong with the approach to prayer that you were given. Of course we feel frustrated—in fact, justifiably hurt and angry—in a relationship in which the other always waits for us to begin the

God Is a Conversation

conversation! In a human relationship it would be intolerable to have to take the initiative in every conversation. The other's refusal to be the first to speak could only be the acting out of passive aggression and glaring evidence of the breakdown of intimacy. Because it feels almost blasphemous to attribute passive aggression to God, however, we often unconsciously absorb our anger and resentment at always having to wait for an answer and take the blame for poor communication upon ourselves. We assume that there is something wrong with us for finding the task of always initiating the conversation with God burdensome; we must lack faith or fervor. This extract from a letter sent by someone who had heard a sermon on prayer is an example of this tendency: "I got your point about sharing feelings with God that I hadn't prayed about. It wasn't easy to put it into words and I felt I was going out on a limb talking to God about it, and asking for help. But I must be doing something wrong because nothing happened. I didn't sense or hear anything. Should I have repeated what I said about myself? I just felt left hanging in the air. . . . Is there something I have missed?" Often our insistence that there is something wrong with the way we pray is a thin veil for resentment of a God whom we have experienced as a passive partner in prayer.

One of the most consistently strange and upsetting features of spiritual life is that feelings which on the surface seem blasphemous and irreligious are in reality inspirations of God and our true allies in the movement of growth and conversion. For example, it is common to censor in prayer expression of our discontentment because it seems more holy to keep up appearances of being grateful and resigned to our

Chapter Two

16

lot. But if God is to shake us from torpor and the acceptance of mediocrity, we need to have our anger kindled. Once expressed, our anger can give way to desire, desire for the new grace which God is goading us to reach for. Time and again the "god" we think we might offend by admitting our real feelings into full consciousness is not God at all, but a projection of ours, an idol either of our own making, or one passed on to us by others. The true God has to be a constant disillusioner, stimulating our discontent and disgust with religious notions and images that are lifeless idols, provoking us to dethrone them. This is why the constant attack on idolatry in the Old Testament never loses its fierce relevance to our lives. The prophets seemed appallingly irreligious to the majority of their contemporaries for daring to launch an all-out attack on sacrosanct religious practices and beliefs.

Prophecy blazed up again in the ministry of Jesus. Passionately devout, learned and observant believers such as the Pharisees were outraged at Jesus for undermining established notions about God that had come to seem secure and unquestionable. They vilified him as a blasphemer. On a small scale the same drama goes on in each one of us. Can we dare to allow our own "twilight of the gods," trusting that the God who is really there will then come through to us? Can it be that the real God is behind thoughts and feelings that seem unspiritual and blameworthy to the part of ourselves that safeguards the status quo?

Paradoxically, weariness and disillusionment with the conventional model of prayer as invariably talking to God and waiting for an answer may be a most promising condition! Contact with the living God can never be wearying.

God Is a Conversation

The weariness with the "passive aggressive" partner is weariness with an idol. The wearier we are with idols the better for God! The hallmark of idols for the prophets was their inertia. They were incapable of taking the initiative. "They have mouths, but they cannot speak; eyes have they, but they cannot see. . . . They have hands, but they cannot feel; feet, but they cannot walk; they make no sound with their throat"(Ps. 115:5,7). They were the passive recipients of devotions and pleadings and sacrifices meant to influence the gods to secure the regularity of seasons and crops.

In complete contrast, Israel's God was all initiative. The living God acted and spoke first, choosing, wooing, calling, inviting. Experience was marked all over with the print of otherness, encounter with unpredictable, uncalled-for, surprising, endlessly versatile action and manifestation. Religion is supremely responsive. The whole of existence, the individual's and the community's, is a conversation which God begins. In prayer, as in life, we are the ones who answer. God touches us, God speaks to us, God moves us, God reveals truth to us, and life and prayer is our response.

In prayer we are never "getting a conversation going" with God. We are continuing a conversation which God has begun. If in a walk by the river my mood of anxious self-preoccupation is broken by a sudden awareness of the beauty of the sunlight reflected in the water, and the swirling of the birds, and I find myself turning to God in a brief expression of praise and appreciation, I am not starting a conversation with God. God spoke first in the language of creation, wooing me back from isolation into belonging and from anxiety into life-giving awareness. Though we seemingly

Chapter Two

open the conversation, our opening is in response to who God has been for us, or what God has done, or is making known to us, or causing us to feel. It sounds at first like a simple adjustment to the conventional definition of prayer that we began with, but in fact for many it amounts to a radical revisioning of the whole enterprise of prayer.

In the first place it gives priority to attention and receptivity. Instead of trying to generate words and feelings to get prayer going, then straining to hear an immediate reply to our opening gambit, paying attention to God's approach to us comes first. Prayer is primarily attentiveness to God's disclosure to us and the heart's response to that disclosure. Furthermore, in much prayer the attention we pay to God's disclosure *is* our response. If, for example, in prayer we are made aware that God loves us as we are, even in our mediocrity, our best response is to savor that, to allow it to sink in, rather than to start to make resolutions and promises to God, which might be a subtle way of changing the subject to what *we* can do. We are loving God, trusting God and uniting ourselves to God precisely by appreciating, savoring, absorbing, realizing, and allowing ourselves to be impregnated with that disclosure of grace. Our contemplative awareness and taking in of God's touch and word is just the "answer" God is hoping for. This answer will gradually get spelled out, not so much by many words in the prayer time, but in the actions and growth that our acceptance of God's disclosure will make possible.

Second, this redefining of prayer compels us to reckon with God as giver and lover, rather than as taskmaster. It is pathetically common for people to be operating under the tacit assumption that prayer is a duty, a requirement, a task. "In order to be a good Christian one must say one's prayers." But how are we to know when we have done enough to satisfy God? Even quite experienced Christians who are hard-working and caring people balk at prayer as yet another demand on top of everything else. Here is another quota to fulfill, this time for a supernatural boss, or another person to satisfy, a super-parent. It seems impossible to summon up the energy for more than a token effort at prayer, but the price for half-hearted and desultory attempts is bad conscience and a dismal estimate of one's worth as a believer. Few people talk about their prayer life without betraying their sense of shame and inadequacy.

What is at fault is rarely laziness, but rather the projecting onto God of the image of the taskmaster. How can there be intimacy with one who is waiting for us to fulfill a quota of prayer-work? Of course prayer will dry up at its source if I assume that it is some kind of performance which I must undertake to be acceptable. My heart will revolt against the demand and I will subconsciously sabotage the whole enterprise of prayer by leaving it until I am too tired, or confining it to those snatched moments in which there is not the slightest chance of going to any depth. But what if this whole game of avoidance is founded on an illusion? What if God does not demand prayer as much as gives prayer? What if God wants prayer in order to satisfy us? What if prayer is a means of God nourishing, restoring, healing, converting us? Suppose prayer is primarily allowing ourselves to be loved, addressed and claimed by God. What if praying means opening ourselves to the gift of God's own self and

Chapter Two

presence? What if our part in prayer is primarily letting God be giver? Suppose prayer is not a duty but the opportunity to experience healing and transforming love? If all this seems utterly obvious to you, be grateful and move on without delay. But if it seems strange or in any way new, pause to take it in. You are far from being unusual if it takes some time to become conscious of your reaction. Perhaps you sense the onset of relief. That oppressive sense of duty could give way. Perhaps the sense of inadequacy and guilt might fade and you could move on to experience reciprocity in prayer, receiving and giving, and thus enter into the realm of spiritual adulthood. Instead of prayer being another demand that threatens to deplete your energy further, it could become the place of replenishment and access to the love which gives life meaning.

There could also be some discomfort because it is not so easy to receive. Receiving means facing our need and accepting dependence on another. It means allowing ourselves to be served and surrendering self-sufficiency. Peter was horrified to find himself looking down at Jesus kneeling before him and preparing to wash his feet. "You shall never wash my feet!" The same reluctance in us resists the idea that prayer is fundamentally receptive.

The next step is to take each aspect of prayer and ask, "How does God make the first move in this? How is God initiating this prayer and drawing me to respond?" Take the example of intercessory prayer. At first it seems like a clear-cut example that justifies the conventional understanding: do I not start by noticing something wrong or someone's need, and then turn to God, asking God to do the best

God Is a Conversation

possible for those I am concerned about?

Deeper reflection alters the picture. God is already in the situation of need, present and active with those who are in want as their upholder and fellow-sufferer. God has reached out to us from that place and touched off a spark of response to that need. Having stimulated our caring, God then recruits our love and concern by stirring us from within to offer that love and concern in intercession. God then receives the love we offer and weaves it into the combined influences which together can bring about the good that God desires.

What about the kind of prayer which is inarticulate, which seems to flounder or consist of mere noises of protest or desire, when we hardly know what we are to offer or what we mean? In fact this very human, raw and incomplete prayer is singled out by St. Paul when he wants to insist that God gives our praying, animates and energizes it. This prayer which is at a loss for words, and seems so poverty-stricken, is the voice of God's own Spirit stirring within the depths of our being! "Likewise the Spirit helps us in our weakness; for we do not know how to pray as we ought, but the Spirit himself intercedes for us with sighs too deep for words. And he who searches the hearts of men knows what is the mind of the Spirit, because the Spirit intercedes for the saints according to the will of God" (Rom. 8:26-27). The prayer that strikes us as meaningless is brimming with meaning to God. At a level deeper than consciousness the Holy Spirit within us is offering our truest needs and desires to the Father.

Chapter Two

The implications of this teaching are very far-reaching. One of the clearest ones is that we have to be extremely careful how we judge and disparage our prayer. It is tempting to assume that prayer is at its best when we are clear and fluent and are aware of feelings of devotion and ardor. But prayer which is much less gratifying to our egos may often be more authentic. Times in prayer when we feel tongue-tied and just murmur words of unadorned need, times when we are plagued by one distraction after another and are reminded of our confusions, times when we experience dryness, rather than being wasted times, are often important ways in which the Spirit takes us into the poverty Christ congratulated in the Beatitudes. These times make us more radically aware of our need and dependence on grace. If we write off these times of prayer we might be despising the gift of God, the very kind of prayer which is best for us at the time, through which God is deeply at work in us. Always regarding prayer as a gift means relinquishing the self-conscious assessment of our own praying, and the anxious tendency to demean our experience.

Second, these words of Paul impress upon us that prayer involves not merely the conscious mind but the depths of the human heart. The upper levels of consciousness register certain aspects of our own inner life and certain signs of God's activity and presence, but only some of them. God is deeply at work within us in ways that are not accessible immediately to consciousness. The Spirit works subliminally at levels deeper than feeling and thought. Unless we are open to this we will be incapable of following the leading of the Spirit in the journey of prayer. We would be likely to

God Is a Conversation

refuse the gift of silence in prayer or the gift of simply "gazing" at the (invisible) wonder of God, because nothing seems to be going on. In fact the spiritual journeys of a great number of people converge on just this territory, in which they are called to an ever more radical trust that God is active even when awareness registers little or nothing. For most of us, faith in this unfelt activity of God in prayer takes time to grow. It is difficult to believe that changes are taking place within us in the dark. But much prayer is like the activity in a photographic dark room: we cannot have the lights on while the process of development is under way.

Perhaps the most elementary kind of prayer is simply calling God by name. Just addressing God. When it is a matter merely of facing God and saying "Father," surely there is no need to go great lengths here and claim that this is God's gift, the response to the Spirit within us and so on. Once again Paul contradicts our tendency to adopt a common sense position. In the same chapter of the Epistle to the Romans he focuses on this simplest of all prayers and claims that it rises out of us because the indwelling Spirit is catching us up into the flow of love that the Risen Christ has for the Father. The Spirit is including us in Christ's experience of the All-embracing One, so we give voice to his own personal name for God, "Abba! Father!" "For you did not receive the spirit of slavery to fall back into fear, but you have received the spirit of sonship. When we cry, 'Abba! Father!' it is the Spirit himself bearing witness with our spirit that we are children of God, and if children, then heirs, heirs of God and fellow heirs with Christ, provided we suffer with him in order that we may also be glorified with him" (Rom. 8:12-17).

This book is going to deal with the form of prayer whose receptive character is unmistakable—meditative prayer. Those who embark on this kind of praying will find themselves before long with little need to be persuaded that God is the initiator and giver in prayer. The experience will be decisive. For in meditative prayer we deliberately open ourselves to hearing God's word to us, sensing God's touch, accepting God's gift and allow ourselves to respond simply to that experience. The particular type of meditative prayer is one that uses the Scriptures as the medium for God's self-disclosure and gift. Meditation on Scripture creates specially favorable conditions for God to speak to us in it and through it, and evoke our response of loving attention, gratitude, of pain, desire, caring, offering, questioning, repenting, trusting, letting go, promising, or whatever it may be.

Now it is tempting simply to reverse the definition we began with and say, "I get it, meditative prayer is a conversation in which I allow God to say something to me through the words and images of the Bible. I take in what God is saying until I really feel its impact, then I respond by expressing my reaction to what God is saying to me and giving to me. In a nutshell, God speaks and I answer." Having said that, it may seem desirable to plunge on and learn some ways to do it. But that would be unwise. There is a danger that this metaphor of conversation between God and the individual will limit our experience.

It is very easy to fall back into a simplistic model of God "out there" speaking to us like another person, and ourselves replying, as in the to and fro of human conversation. It exerts a tremendous pull on us. So much so that when we hear Scripture speak of the Holy Spirit present and active in the heart, and of how we are united with the Ascended Christ and are taken up into his life and drawn into his intimacy with the Father, all this stays with us for only a moment and is soon replaced by the dominant conventional image of direct, one-on-one *confrontation* with God. Remaining within the confines of this image of prayer as a one-on-one confrontation will prevent us from breaking through to the distinctly Christian experience of God.

The distinctive Christian experience of God is expressed in Trinitarian worship and Trinitarian belief. The church came to know that it could not do justice to Christian experience by regarding the New Testament images of the indwelling Spirit, of union with the only-begotten Son, of intimacy in him with the All-embracing One, Abba, as merely colorful metaphors which enliven our devotion to the One God. Prayer, worship, and the life of the Christian community lead to a radical revisioning of who God is, a revolutionizing of our grasp of God's identity as daring today as it was almost two thousand years ago. The experience we call Christian orthodoxy insists that we cannot have a one-on-one confrontation with God because God is not merely one. God is a three-fold life—Trinity! The "personal" God of Christian experience is not an omnipotent Individual, but a communion of self-giving love.

We hold before us the scene of Jesus being baptized in the Jordan, the Spirit descending on him and the voice of the Father heard acclaiming him as the Son, and we ask, "Where is God here?" The church came to realize that God was to be recognized and worshipped on every side of the relationships the scene displays symbolically. The unique relationship of Jesus and the One he called Father has revealed to us an eternal relationship within the Being of God. From all eternity God has had another Self to receive and return love perfectly and express the Divine Creativity. It was that Self, the Eternal Word, which was free to embrace our humanity by becoming a human being in Jesus. The relationship of the Father and Spirit who descends and fills Jesus reveals a relationship within the Being of God. From all eternity God has had another Self to communicate and give the divine life. The Breath of God is God, God pouring forth to enliven and restore creation to its Source. God is the name we give to the One who loves and gives, the One who is loved and endowed, the One who is gift and love. God is the name for the Father, the Son, and the Holy Spirit. But words continually fail us here. The astonishing vision of God as communion of love and self-giving cannot be captured in words and definitions.

When we encounter God there is no individual to confront. For we encounter and are drawn into relationship, reciprocity, the dynamism of mutual love and self-giving going on within God. Utterly unlike the splendid isolation of the "Supreme Being" of conventional monotheism, the life of the Trinity known in Christian worship and prayer has within itself the fullness of what we experience in community, intimacy and sacrificial love!

Are you prepared to trust this way of envisaging God? It is the faith of the church, it arose out of spiritual experience, not speculation, and it has been constantly renewed through the centuries in spiritual experience. It is presented now, not as a test of traditional belief, but as a key to your past and potential experience. It is one thing to say that prayer is a conversation with God. It is another to say that God begins the conversation. But it is yet something else to say that *God is a conversation.* In God love ever flows between the Father and the Son in the Spirit. Love is answered by love, and the conversation, the utter opposite of *"égoisme à deux,"* takes in the suffering of a whole universe striving to attain fulfillment with its Creator. Prayer is already going on in God. In the love the All-embracing Father has for the Son, and in the love the Son has for the Father, in the issuing of the Spirit from the Father and the Spirit's return in the love of the Son, there is everything we mean by prayer—intimacy, adoration, self-offering, love, desire, crucifyingly acute sympathy for a world torn by pain and joy. Our prayer is not making conversation with God. It is joining the conversation that is already going on in God. It is being invited to participate in the relationships of intimacy between Father, Son and Holy Spirit. There is an eternal dance already in full swing, and we are caught up in to it. Prayer is allowing ourselves to join the dance and experience the movements, the constant interplay of the Persons of the Trinity.

Experience will confirm this for you. Already these images of prayer and God, which are not the standard fare provided from most pulpits, may already be working some change in your feelings. Perhaps you are sensing that past inhibitions in prayer may well have been linked with an oppressive discomfort at being asked to address Almighty God across a gulf of utter otherness. Now comes the chance to experience prayer as an intimacy with God already available to us which we can experience by letting down our defenses, disarming ourselves. At the same time you may be realizing that this availability of intimacy raises the issue of our fear of intimacy. A formal relationship with "Almighty God" may be heavy-going, but it does maintain the distance our unhealed selves want to keep.

That we want intimacy with God cannot be taken for granted. We need to do some more pondering about what as human beings we are really looking for in our quest for relationship. What sort of fulfillment are we to expect in our relationships with God? How does God meet our deepest needs, and what part does meditative prayer play in this fulfillment? These are the questions we go on to consider in the next chapter.

3

Who Do You Think You Are, To Enter This Conversation?

The idea of prayer as the conversation of love which takes place in God, in which we are invited to participate, is a rather daring one. When we do something daring we often get challenged, and it is fascinating that the challenge is frequently issued in the form of a question about our identity. "What do you think you are doing? Where do you think you are going?" we are asked. But often the challenge takes the form, "Who do you think you are? Who do you think you are to ask me that personal question?" It is a rhetorical question we can address to ourselves, too. If I fall in love with someone who seems unattainably beyond my reach I might find myself writing in my journal, "Who on earth do I think I am to dream of winning the love of someone like her?"

All the great questions of life can be asked in these simple, everyday forms. Who do we think we are, to assume we can be drawn into the flow of love between Jesus, the All-embracing One whom he called "Abba," and the Spirit? Who do you think you are? This is the great question with regard to prayer. How we pray is not a matter of some technique or style. It derives from our deepest sense of personal identity. How I pray flows from who I think I am.

The question of identity invites answers on two levels. One level is that of particularity and individuality. What makes me unique? What constitutes my distinctive personality? Self-knowledge of this kind is encouraged in Christian spirituality because we believe in a Creator who is responsible for the infinity of variables which make every human creature unique, and delights in diversity. In the life of prayer I become more and more aware of the uniqueness of my relationship with God because I am different from any other human being. The other level is that of personhood, rather than personality. Who do I think I am *as a human being?* What does it mean to be a person? This is the level it is especially worth exploring as we begin to go deeper into considering prayer. Who do I think I am? How am I built? What am I eligible for? What makes me tick as a person? What potentialities are there in me, just by being human, for relating to God?

We can do justice to these questions without getting overwhelmed with complex philosophical and psychological issues by focusing on the theme of relationships. In the last few decades, research into the psychological development of infants by such pioneers as Margaret Mahler has encouraged us to think of the personhood of the newborn baby as still potential, not realized for a number of months. At first the infant is merged and fused with the encompassing world of the mother's being, without any sense of differentiation or self-identity. It is only in time that the intense attention and care of the mother evokes a sense of self in the baby. This mysterious differentiation in which the infant becomes more aware of herself as distinct is such a wonderful and crucial event that we are learning to speak of it as the second birth of the infant. We emerge from this second birth into the realm of mutuality and reciprocity. The achievement of personhood is developed and consolidated in the mystery of communication through language. If this "normal miracle" of development goes according to plan, the new person embarks on a lifetime drama of relating to others. In every case the plot is determined by our ineradicable yearning for two fundamental kinds of experiences; on the one hand for the experience of being accompanied by others, in communion with them, included, held, and on the other hand for the experience of independence and distinctness with initiative all our own.

Carlo Levi, a brilliant Italian artist, writer and doctor, summed up this way of understanding the constitution of our humanness by defining personhood as "*il luogo di tutti rapporti,*" the meeting place of all our relationships. Even crude and unreflective popular parlance testifies to the same intuition that it is in our relationships and in mutuality that our personhood resides; when some neurological calamity or mental illness robs a human being of all capacity to respond to others the terrible phrase "just a vegetable" is often heard. It is a repulsive usage, but one that expresses an authentic horror at the fact that while we still draw breath personhood, in the sense of our capacity for conscious relationship, can go into abeyance.

Now when a Christian explores the question "Who do I think I am *as a human being?*" he does it with the map and compass of Christian doctrine, in particular with the teach-

Chapter Three

ing that human beings are made "in the image and likeness of God." The wording derives from the first chapter of Genesis, "So God created man in his own image, in the image of God he created him; male and female he created them." This profound and daring teaching was built into their narrative of creation by priestly writers of the Jewish communities exiled in Babylon. It appears that as they considered how the pagan gods had their images and likenesses in the form of idols, mere artifacts of wood and metal, they realized that the unique and all-powerful God they knew, the living God, could find visible, tangible expression in the world only in the forms of living persons made for relationship and faithful intimacy. The experience of Jesus Christ opened up new depths in the doctrine. Human beings did not have merely a faint trace of the divine character. The potential we had been endowed with for reflecting God's own life was so high that "in the fullness of time" God could perfectly express God's own self in human terms in the person of Jesus. God's eternal self-expression or Word was able to be "made flesh."

We need quite a bit of guidance in exploring this theme of being created in the image and likeness of God because it is easy to wander off in directions that lead nowhere. For example, it is tempting to suppose that each individual is to be thought of as a miniature reproduction of God, so to speak. Then God is thought of as the original Mighty Individual, a gigantically powerful Super-person. In fact this is what countless numbers of religious people implicitly believe. Religion is a matter of the individual relating to a Supreme Being. This is to make God in the image and likeness of our fallen selves, attributing to God our broken-ness as separated individuals. But authentic Christianity is very different. It teaches that the places where we are to discern the signs of God's being are in the patterns of our personal relatedness, our mutuality and reciprocity, our lives of community and intimacy, our "intercourse"—that is why the ancient writers insisted that the image of God lay along the male/female axis of sexual diversity and sexual union, "male and female he created them."

One way of imagining the question of image and likeness is to think of a lock and the key made to fit it. A key and its lock do not look like each other, one is not a big version of the other. But a key is made after the image and likeness of the lock, it fits and meshes with it, it belongs in it and its purpose and destiny is to move in it. We are not miniatures of God (we are in fact a strange kind of ape!) but our mysterious evolution influenced by the Spirit working in creation has made us able to "fit" the being of God, our beings match and mesh with God's. Our deepest needs as persons are met and fulfilled by who God actually is. Every aspect of ourselves as persons-in-relationship is blessed and completed by contact and union with all that God is.

Let us consider then the three basic ways in which we need to enter into relationship in order to be fully human. After the second birth we discussed earlier, which brings self-awareness, we enter into relationship with all that is not us, all that has given us life, all upon which we depend. We did not choose to be born, we were thrown into life, and are utterly dependent on the physical and human environment that sustains us. In the immediate foreground there is mother, and then around her father, and other caretakers and family members, teachers and so on. There is the setting of life itself, the light and air, the ground and sky, liquid and solid. Soon we must relate to this All, this Whole. On the one hand our experience is partly good; there is enough sustenance, comfort, stimulus and security for us to feel that we belong, that we can actively respond to life itself, to our world, with trust. But we have negative experience also of frustration, neglect, even abuse, danger, and pain. Some people so live into this dark experience that life itself seems hostile and the world capricious and menacing. They respond with mistrust, withdrawal or rebellion. At one extreme there are those who come to be in love with life, vibrantly involved and intensely appreciative of the adventure of living. At the other there are the lonely and alienated, those who are lost in the world and cut off from its meaning, so out of relationship with the Whole that suicide seems the only way to express their situation of abandonment. And between the extremes there is a huge spectrum of responses in which love of life and fear of life are in ever-fluctuating tension. To be fully human we need to find our relatedness to the Whole, to Life itself.

The second way we need to be in relationship is partnership. We need to choose others to keep us company in the journey of life, and we need others to choose us. As we grow up we feel our way into the quest for intimacy and find a measure of confidence in ourselves that we can be found desirable as partners to another, and can take initiative in wooing those others. The need for intimacy is primarily fulfilled for most people in marriage, but there are other human journeys in which friends or members of a community are the significant companions on the way. It is not enough to be stuck with others accidentally or merely thrown into association with a group. We need to choose and be chosen to satisfy this deep need for reciprocity and mutuality in life. If no one chooses me, and I am impotent to choose others, the result is a half-life of quiet desperation.

The third basic level of relatedness is with myself. In a mysterious way I must enter into relationship with my own unique being, my own self. Every thought is a kind of conversation or dialogue with myself; everyone converses silently or aloud with himself or herself. But from another point of view it is an adventure to really love and accept ourselves in depth by entering into conversation with the voices of our inner world, respecting and cherishing and recognizing the strange depths within which our deepest feelings have their roots. Many people do not choose to be in relationship with themselves more than superficially out of unwillingness to face mysteries within themselves, or from basic self-hatred. Many people feel cut off from themselves, unable to know why they behave as they do, or what is the source of their anxiety, fear and malaise. But in order to be fully human we need to be healed of this alienation from the self, and come to embrace all that we are.

What is distinctively good about the good news of the Christian gospel is that the Living God is all we could possibly hope God to be. God meets us in each of the three aspects of our need. The Trinity of Love fulfills our threefold longing to be united to the Whole, to be chosen in love and empowered to choose and love in return, to be reconciled and healed within ourselves.

We cry out for reunion with the Whole of Life. God the Father is the All, in whom all things live and move and have their being. By being reconciled to the Father through Christ, by letting him draw us into the arms of the All-Embracing One, we find ourselves beginning to love the creation in which we belong.

We cry out to be found and chosen, for company and partnership in the strange adventure of human living and dying. God the Son chose us in compassion and entered our life as the Son of man, died for us, plunging to the depths of our sinfulness and estrangement. In the Resurrection he is given to us as the Partner we long for, the Companion who will never desert us. He includes us in the community of his Body, the church, and sets us the task of emancipating others from every kind of bondage.

We cry out to have life within ourselves, the power to love freely, the ability to give and create, for wholeness within ourselves. God is given to us as the Holy Spirit dwelling in the depths of our being, overcoming our alienation from self, enabling us to love ourselves and our neighbors as ourselves.

Prayer is communion between all that we are and all that God is. Therefore prayer always involves our needs at these three levels. God is always active in us in all three ways. Prayer takes place at the meeting place of these three paths of relationship. There can be no prayer unless the Spirit is actively engaging the depths of our heart and stirring us from within. There can be no prayer which bypasses the human relationship we have with Jesus. There can be no prayer which does not open us to the Ultimate Mystery of the One who is Love and "is above all and through all and in all" (Eph. 4:6).

The pattern of this experience of intimacy with God in prayer is expressed with particular clarity in a passage from the Letter to the Ephesians: "For this reason I bow my knees before the Father, from whom every family in heaven and on earth is named, that according to the riches of his glory he may grant you to be strengthened with might through his Spirit in the inner man, and that Christ may dwell in your hearts through faith; that you, being rooted and grounded in love, may have power to comprehend with all the saints what is the breadth and length and height and depth, and to know the love of Christ which surpasses knowledge, that you may be filled with all the fullness of God" (3:14-19).

The writer of this letter, possibly a disciple of Paul, longs for his readers to enter into the fullest experience of God's presence and this involves the three dimensions we have been considering. He wants them to experience the gift of strength in their hearts, the energy, richness and sense of identity that comes from recognizing that the Spirit of God is at home and at work deep within. He wants them to experience the way the Spirit within makes real the living presence of Christ. From this faith experience of relationship with the living Christ they will find themselves putting roots down into the rich, nourishing soil of love. They will begin to experience an expansion of their sense of meaning and grasp of life in every direction as they enter into relationship with the Father whose love is limitless and who connects everything. Ultimately they will come to know that this Life of all life is within their very selves in all its fullness, not merely "out there," or away in heaven.

The passage is itself a prayer, and concludes with the offering of praise to the One who "by the power at work within us is able to do far more abundantly than all that we ask or think," so it is entirely appropriate to take it as a basic model for prayer, in particular the kind of meditative prayer we are dealing with in this book. It is precisely in this kind of prayer that we sink roots into love and open ourselves to the power of God at work within us.

We need to consider how in and through meditation with Scripture our inmost selves are touched and shaped by meeting the humanness of God's Word, and how we open ourselves to the mystery of All-Embracing Love. This we will do in the chapter that follows. Just now it is worth pausing to reflect why it is so important to dwell on these questions of human identity and the Christian doctrine of the Trinity. Prayer taught as a technique is valueless. We could toy with certain methods of praying with Scripture passages for a while, but unless we are prepared to go to the root of what we expect and desire in our relationship with God prayer will soon wither. A superficial competence in certain spiritual techniques is short-lived and valueless. What counts is our readiness to explore for ourselves at first hand the mystery of God, the God revealed in Good Friday, Easter and Pentecost.

4

The Trinity In Our Praying With Scripture

One of my favorite definitions of prayer comes from a saint of the Eastern Church, St. Gregory of Sinai: "Prayer is God, who worketh all things in man." It is deceptively simple and we have needed several chapters already to explore some of its implications. Prayer is God at work within us, stimulating and enabling our response of faith and love. All prayer arises from God's working within us, all prayer draws us into the love which flows between the persons of the Trinity. In this chapter we now sharpen the focus on the particular form of prayer to which this book is devoted. What is the pattern of God's presence as Father, Son and Spirit in our meditating with Scripture? We begin by reflecting on the activity of the Spirit in meditation.

THE SPIRIT IN THE HEART

"On the last day of the feast, the great day, Jesus stood up and proclaimed, 'If any one thirst, let him come to me and drink. He who believes in me, as the scripture has said, "Out of his heart shall flow rivers of living water.'" Now this he said about the Spirit, which those who believed in him were to receive; for as yet the Spirit had not been given, because Jesus was not yet glorified" (John 7:37-39).

Jesus is shown in this passage comparing the presence of the Spirit in the depths of the self to the flow of a never-failing river. Perhaps this image came from his own experience after being filled with the Spirit at his baptism by John in the Jordan. The evangelist has already shown Jesus telling the Samaritan woman at the well that he was able to give to others this experience of the inner spring of life: "Whoever drinks of the water that I shall give him will never thirst; the water that I shall give him will become in him a spring of water welling up to eternal life" (John 4:14).

How are we to understand the expression "out of the heart?" The heart is the commonest image in Scripture for the spiritual core and center of the human person and the translators of the Revised Standard Version have used it here to translate a Greek word for which the nearest English equivalent is "guts." *Koilia* means the viscera, the inner organs, including the womb. It is a robust, earthy word and the King James version translates it vividly with the word "belly." Our modern talk about the spiritual center or soul of a person can indicate a tendency to retreat to a rather intellectual and abstract plane. Scripture offers us very concrete, fleshy images which challenge us to view the human person as thoroughly embodied. The ancient Hebrews located the human passions and desires and needs not only in the heart but the kidneys and liver and other inner organs. So to talk of the Spirit rising up like a river in the guts is to

The Trinity in Our Praying with Scripture

claim that the Spirit actively engages not merely our lofty ideals and intellectual processes but our deepest cravings, instincts, needs and energies.

In the background of this image is the first appearance of the Spirit right at the beginning of Genesis, upon which Jesus had no doubt often meditated. "The earth was without form and void, and darkness was upon the face of the deep; and the Spirit of God was moving over the face of the water." The Breath of God, the Wind of God, is seen brooding over and stirring the chaos which is the raw material of the word which is coming to be. And the Spirit is not only involved in the unformed, primal levels of our feelings and energies, but in the distorted, wounded and misdirected energies that give rise to evil thoughts and actions. "For from within, out of the heart of man, come evil thoughts, fornication, theft, murder, adultery, coveting, wickedness, deceit, licentiousness, envy, slander, pride, foolishness. All these evil things come from within, and they defile a man" (Mark 7:21-23). The Spirit cannot keep out of the heart until all is well and we are pure enough. The Spirit wells up in the heart in order to bring love and reconciliation to these ruined or sick elements in ourselves.

Another thing to notice about these passages is the association of the Holy Spirit with desire. The Spirit comes in response to deep desire, to thirst. When Jesus promises that the one who drinks the water he shall give will never thirst, he of course does not mean that desire will be numbed and abolished. He does not promise an anaesthetic, but that this basic longing for fulfillment will be met, and will go on being met by the indwelling Spirit. Scripture presents the Spirit as the awakener of desire, and desire as a gift impelling us towards God. This theme marks the closing page of Scripture, as its last word to us: "The Spirit and the Bride say, 'Come.' And let him who hears say, 'Come.' And let him who is thirsty come, let him who *desires* take the water of life without price" (Rev. 22:17).

Meditative prayer "in the Spirit" then will have these two qualities. It will be a kind of praying that does not confine itself to the surface levels of reasoning and talking and thinking. It won't be a matter of the head, and tidy, controlled conversations with the Lord. This kind of praying will involve the inner world where the invisible springs of our actions lie, it will penetrate to levels of deep need, disturbance, feeling, levels where we are hurt and warped, and levels where we have wants not at all satisfied by conventional palliatives, and gifts waiting to come out of bud. Second, this kind of praying will be energized by tapping a basic desire for fulfillment, a desire to be found desirable by God, a desire for God, a kind of longing and loving without limits.

Now what the biblical writers mean by the heart includes what contemporary thought refers to as the psyche. This is not the place for building up a grand psychological theory, but there is one basic insight about the human psyche that throws light on the practice of meditative prayer with Scripture. The language of the psyche is the language of *symbol*. The most obvious disclosure of this truth takes place every single night when we dream. In the thoroughly mysterious activity of dreaming, while the waking mind is in suspense, the unconscious mind processes our past and current experiences in highly charged symbolic dramas. Appearing in our dreams are classic personages, or archetypes, found apparently in virtually every culture, symbols that seem to be native to the human heart everywhere. Mingled with them are characters and images that carry the impressions of our own personal history and experience. Every human being is a natural virtuoso in dreaming; we are intrinsically equipped with the capacity for weaving endless dramas saturated in symbolic significance. They tend to remain opaque to the kind of reasoning we do in the cold light of day and most people ignore them; it takes imagination and care to attend to the symbols thrown up in our dreams.

Whether we interpret our dreams or not, dreaming tells us something tremendously important. It tells us that the psyche is a kind of switchboard for conveying meaning, and it makes the connection through symbols. Desires, needs, instincts from the most basic level of our nature as living organisms are clothed in symbolic forms so that they can be identified and reckoned with and used by our reasons. Blind, inarticulate feelings and processes are handed on up to the spirit and mind after having been transposed into images and symbols. The switchboard also operates to connect messages coming from above, as it were. The deep levels of the self are built to respond not to rational concepts but to images and symbols. If our feelings are to be moved and our energies harnessed, abstractions are powerless. Symbols are needed in order to penetrate and activate the deepest layers of our being. The psyche which "throws symbols up" from below also takes them in from above and activates the connections which lead to inner transformations or galvanizes us into action.

The Scriptures are a vast treasury of potent symbols embodying God's revelation. They contain range upon range of mythic themes, metaphors and images. Most of the historical narratives are not mere records but stories remembered and retold precisely because they were pregnant with symbolic significance and revelatory, sacramental, transforming power. Meditative prayer with Scripture is the art of absorbing, taking in image after image of Scripture so that the Spirit within us can impress the deepest levels of our being with their meaning. In meditative prayer the Spirit makes the connection between our deepest needs and the images that answer them and convey the grace and touch of God's power. In meditating on the images of Scripture our inarticulate feelings find expression for themselves so that they can come to the surface and be consciously offered to God. And again as we meditate on the images of Scripture and take them in at the inner level of the heart, we allow ourselves to be touched and moved and transformed. Guiding and enabling this process of connecting through symbols is the Spirit, the self-effacing, inner Giver of Meaning.

According to the Gospel of John, Jesus taught the disciples to expect that his words would only really come home to them when they had received the indwelling Spirit. Only the Spirit could interpret their meaning and bring them to life. "The Counsellor, the Holy Spirit, whom the Father will send in my name, he will teach you all things, and bring to your remembrance all that I have said to you. . . . He will guide you into all the truth; for he will not speak on his own authority, but whatever he hears he will speak, and he will

The Trinity in Our Praying with Scripture

declare to you the things that are to come. He will glorify me, for he will take what is mine and declare it to you" (John 14:26;16:13,14). Of course, the outstanding characteristic of Jesus' teaching is its embodiment in symbols. "With many such parables he spoke the word to them, as they were able to hear it; he did not speak to them without a parable," commented Mark (4:33,34). And the Jesus of John's gospel speaks all the time in pregnant imagery: I am the light of the world, the true vine, the living bread, and so on. It is through the Spirit in the heart that these "words of life" come to life in us and for us.

THE ENCOUNTER WITH JESUS
IN MEDITATIVE PRAYER

After praying that they may be "strengthened with might through his Spirit in the inner man," the writer to the Ephesians next prayed that Christ may dwell in their hearts through faith. The Spirit is there not to claim our attention but to give us the living presence of Christ and bring us into relationship with him. In meditating with Scripture we are exploring our relationship with Christ.

The practice of meditative prayer is based on the fundamental Christian belief that Christ is the Word of God, God's self-expression. "In many and various ways God spoke of old to our fathers by the prophets; but in these last days he has spoken to us by a Son, whom he appointed heir of all

Chapter Four

things, through whom also he created the world. He reflects the glory of God and bears the very stamp of his nature, upholding the universe by his word of power" (Heb. 1:1-3). Conversation with God is primarily paying attention to what God is saying; and what God is saying is what God has already said in Jesus. Meditative prayer is listening to the Word in the faith that this Word-made-flesh, Jesus Christ, is what God has to say about us and about God's self. God continues to speak in many and various ways, but none of these words can cancel or replace what God was and is communicating by the life and ministry, the rejection and death, the resurrection and glorification of Jesus. The essence of meditative prayer is letting the word of Christ dwell in us richly (Col. 3:16).

Another image which will be important in our exposition of one of the methods of meditative prayer comes from the eucharist. The Anglican eucharistic liturgy speaks of "feeding on him in our hearts by faith with thanksgiving." Meditation is a way of taking Christ into our lives as nourishment. Yet another image, given by Paul in the Second Epistle to the Corinthians, is that of gazing on Christ. Prayer is looking at Jesus, the image of God, with such singleness of heart and receptivity that we become irradiated by his glory, and begin to reflect it. "And we all, with unveiled face, beholding the glory of the Lord, are being changed into his likeness from one degree of glory to another; for this comes from the Lord who is the Spirit" (3:18). This will be an important theme when we consider contemplative prayer with images from Scripture.

What it is essential to grasp is that this receiving of the

gift of God's revelation in Jesus is not at all like soaking up the benefit of a past event, or allowing oneself to be inspired by a hero through admiring meditation on his deeds and character. Christ is alive, and it is the living contemporary Christ making himself known to us by means of the stories and words of his life handed on from the past. It is Christ in us meeting us through the stories and words of Scripture. The difference is revealed by the freedom to speak to Christ in our hearts in prayer.

Many people balk at the suggestion that we should pray to Christ. Again and again the protest is heard that we should pray only to God (meaning the Father). Sometimes misgivings about praying to Jesus are simply the result of rather poor teaching of Christian doctrine. But sometimes they are felt strongly because the issue of prayer to Christ really tests our belief in the resurrection. If people are basically unsure here, that uncertainty need not emerge in prayer because they can carry on praying away to the Father, and Christ can be left out of the picture. At the end of the prayer the formula "in the name of Jesus Christ" can be added, rather like putting a stamp on a parcel. It is a relief to be told that one should only pray to "the Almighty," then one doesn't ever have to come right out in the open and face up to the problem one has in believing whether Jesus is actually there for us.

There is no suggestion in the New Testament that the conversation with the Risen Christ that his followers had when he appeared to them ceased abruptly with the last of those special appearances. In fact one of the earliest Christian prayers, preserved in Aramaic, the language of Jesus and the disciples, is "Maranatha, Our Lord, come!" This is prayer addressed to Jesus. Even in the public worship of the church, there was no suggestion that prayer was to be exclusively directed to the Father.

The Spirit in the heart brings the living Christ into the heart and we are not to remain mute in this presence. Every inhibition is to be firmly rejected. We are meant to speak with him in self-disclosure, love and praise.

The Scriptures are especially insistent that Jesus is present to us in continuing human companionship. The Risen Christ showed the wounds of his torture and execution to his disciples. His humanity has not been erased by his glorification. He hasn't dissolved into an abstract spiritual principle, some vague, genderless "Eternal Christ." "Jesus Christ is the same yesterday, today and for ever," the Epistle to the Hebrews proclaims (13:8). This letter keeps on reminding us of Jesus' human vulnerability. "In the days of his flesh, Jesus offered up prayers and supplications, with loud cries and tears, to him who was able to save him from death, and he was heard for his godly fear. Although he was a Son, he learned obedience through the things he suffered" (5:7,8). The more we grasp that Jesus is still utterly human, the more we accept our humanity and pray out of our vulnerability, precariousness and dependence. "Since then we have a great priest who has passed through the heavens, Jesus, the Son of God, let us hold fast our confession. For we have not a high priest who is unable to sympathize with our weaknesses, but one who in every respect has been tempted as we are, yet without sinning. Let us then with confidence draw near to the throne of grace, that we may receive mercy

The Trinity in Our Praying with Scripture

and find grace to help in time of need" (4:14-16).

Meditative prayer which focuses on Jesus constantly brings us back from our spiritual evasions and makes us deal with the real issues of our lives, our relationships, our sexuality, our feelings, our needs, our hurts, our desires. The one who called himself the Human Being (the conventional, literal translation is "The Son of man") always addresses and challenges us in our humanity, the real context in which we actually struggle, suffer and try to flourish, but which we are often tempted to leave behind in prayer.

The Word became flesh in Jesus, proclaims the Gospel of John. But this taking up of our humanity by God, wasn't an utter bolt from the blue, completely unrelated to all God's communication before. The Old Testament Scriptures witness to a God who wrestles with men and women, struggling with them in the tangle of their messy lives, embracing them in their weakness and ambiguity. Think of the dealings of God with Jacob, to name only one man! The early believers did not throw their Jewish Scriptures away after the ascension. Just the opposite, they pored over them with redoubled intensity, and found that the Risen Christ opened their eyes to find him "between the lines" of all the holy books. The story of the appearance of Jesus to the couple going to Emmaus captures the sense of discovery: "And beginning with Moses and all the prophets, he interpreted to them in all the scriptures the things concerning himself" (Luke 24:27). This means that Christ present in the heart is able to use not only the stories and words of Scripture which explicitly refer to him to heal and convert us. The whole range of Scripture is open to him as the means of provoking, enlightening, engaging our humanness, and stimulating our faith in him and love of the Holy One. In meditation on the Old Testament Scriptures we are not temporarily bypassing our union with Christ. They are means of stimulating and deepening our awareness of the outrageous humanity of God, who gets into the fray of human lives as our lover and rescuer, instead of remaining in the remoteness of heaven.

THE EMBRACE OF THE FATHER

The passage from Ephesians we are using to explore the nature of meditative prayer tells us that the essence of prayer is coming to "know the love of Christ which surpasses knowledge." In prayer we expose ourselves to God's love in Christ, and allow ourselves to experience it. Without this actual experience, the love of Christ remains a mere concept, an idea. The greatest expression of Christ's love is his gift to us of a share in his relationship with "Abba," the All-embracing One. It is not a love which leaves us where we are, but one which takes us into his intimacy with the Mystery who gave us birth. Prayer does not lead to any kind of fixation on the person of Jesus. The movement of desire does not come to a halt there. Instead we find ourselves turned with him in the direction in which he gazes, that is into the face of the utter mystery of God which can never be pinned down or captured. Experiencing Christ's love turns us towards the horizon of the Infinitely Wonderful with whom he is completely in love. The goal of prayer is to enter

The Trinity in Our Praying with Scripture

into the condition of being unrestrainedly in love with God. The encounter in prayer with the Father is not therefore a matter of coming up against a figure, or a being. It is the experience of the falling away of the constraints, the restrictions, the cramping inhibitions which limit our love. In Christ we begin little by little to experience liberation from the narrowness and pettiness and fear which bottle us up in the confines of individual life. In prayer our horizons broaden in every direction, "that you, being rooted and grounded in love, may have power to comprehend with all the saints what is the breadth and length and height and depth."

We can take height and depth to indicate the gradual discovery within ourselves of unfathomable and limitless desire. If we are prepared to do without too many narcotics in life it eventually teaches us, with much pain and disillusionment, that even when we love wonderful people and enjoy the best gifts the world offers, they do not quite satisfy our longing for fulfillment or take away our inner loneliness. In prayer we can finally give free rein to that desire. Sharing the experience of Jesus, we discover that our limitless desire is utterly appropriate since we have a limitless Object of desire who desires us. Nowhere on earth can we love without qualification, without certain restraints. But sharing the experience of Jesus, our loving is oriented towards the All-Embracing One and we can take off the brakes, abandon all restraint. We can adore. We can worship. We can admire absolutely. We can entrust ourselves unhesitating. We can throw off every inhibition. We discover, sharing the experience of Jesus, that this is the very secret of becoming a free person. Only there is no thing to fantasize about, or "person" to imagine in this encounter with the One Jesus called Abba. The "Father" is not a figure for our fantasy but a mystery before which our capacity to love unrestrainedly opens up. So time and again meditative prayer with Scripture ends in silence, in desiring, in wanting, in yearning, in just being there, in finding ourselves free to love God without having a thing to hold on to or look at. In other words, meditation flows into contemplation.

There are the horizontal dimensions of breadth and length. Prayer brings me out of isolation and situates me in the community embraced by God. Instead of my inner loneliness making me feel hopelessly solitary, I experience it as the very thing I have in common with the whole company of God-seekers. I know I belong to them, that we are in this together. Notice how the Scripture passage from Ephesians asks for "the power to comprehend *with all the saints* what is the breadth and length and height and depth." Gradually I find that prayer puts all my wants and needs into the widest context. Instead of being imprisoned in self-obsession I begin to discover that what I suffer and desire is part of what *we* undergo and strive for. The feelings prayer allows me to express draw me into solidarity with my fellow human beings. They give voice to our experience. I am not alone.

True prayer wears down my indifference and self-containment. Community becomes what I care about more than anything—community for us all, with no one left outside. The Father before whom we bow our knees, to use Paul's words, we find to be the One "from whom every family in heaven and on earth is named." Everyone is meant to flourish in just

The Trinity in Our Praying with Scripture

communities sustained by God. Everyone is invited into the community-in-making which Jesus called the kingdom of God. So prayer in the presence of the Father makes me care more and more about the struggle for just communities and the promise of that ultimate community. I am drawn into the breadth and length of God's embrace in prayer and nothing could be less like the "flight of the alone to the Alone." It is the attraction of the lonely into the community which is in God. And here we end with the primary focus of Jesus' own prayer. "Father, your kingdom come!" His heart opened up in the presence of the All-Embracing One, Jesus yearns for the realization of the community meant for all humanity. All true prayer draws us into that yearning. Meditation leads us not only to contemplation but to intercession and to the offering of ourselves for action for the fulfillment of God's will in the world.

5

God Touching Us Through The Scriptures

In meditative prayer I give God an opportunity to begin a new conversation with myself by entering one of the conversations now embedded in our Scriptures. The Bible is a vast web of interwoven conversations, encounters of faith and struggle and disclosure between God and men and women. Much of it is hard to read. To us now many of the conversations are obscure. Some of them are offensive. Yet as we become familiar with them we find ourselves drawn into more and more of them. In prayer I put myself into one of those conversations and this stimulates my own receptivity and response to God now. God uses the historic faith encounter to draw me into my own today.

It is exciting to discover that this process by which God uses old stories, old records of faith encounter, to speak again in new ways to new people, is found in the Scriptures themselves. The words of particular prophets addressed to certain historical situations were recorded, but instead of being discarded when new situations arose, they were revised and reapplied in order to stimulate faith and hope in the new generation of believers. The books of the prophets were edited again and again to make their proclamations of God's love and judgment come alive in new settings. For example, once the kingdom of Israel had met its doom, the disciples of the northern prophet Hosea did not bury their collections of his sayings in archives. They gave them a new lease of life by substituting references to Judah in some of the places where he had originally spoken of Israel, so that the people in the southern kingdom could take his message to heart. After the Jews had returned from exile in Babylon they added an optimistic prediction of restoration to Amos' prophecies of doom so that they could see their own experience reflected in the venerable book and make it newly their own. Editors and historians compiling traditional stories wove them together in new ways so they could inspire their contemporaries in their struggle with fresh issues. The early Christians retold the stories of Jesus' ministry and reworked his teachings in order to bring out their meaning and power for new believers living in different contexts from the original witnesses.

Biblical scholars have many techniques for uncovering the process by which communities of faith entered into a new dialogue with God on the basis of stories and traditions which they had received from the past and then handed these on in fresh versions which reflect their experience of God. It would be absurd to suppose that one has to be versed in these techniques in order to be eligible to pray with the Bible. On the other hand it is equally false to reject biblical criticism out of hand and consider it an enemy of prayer. The attitudes cultivated in meditative prayer and the fundamental tenets of Scripture scholarship are compatible. They have in common the belief that God's word is not a compendium of timeless, unchanging messages which different people have to apply to themselves as best they can. Prayer and scholarship know that God deals with people where they are in all their particularity and uniqueness. As we approach the Scriptures to use them in prayer it is good to be as aware as possible of the historical circumstances which gave rise to the Scriptures in their present form. At the same time we recognize that our situation is also unique. God can use the Scripture to speak to us personally in our new setting and circumstances.

Suppose I have been reading the Gospel of John and meditating in turn on passages that intrigue me and attract me. Now I have come to the final chapter and open myself to what God might be saying to me through it. This twenty-first chapter contains the story of Peter and a group of disciples doing a night's fishing back in Galilee in the early days after Jesus' resurrection. A stranger on the shore advises them after they have caught nothing all night. After they make a magnificent catch of fish, they recognize the stranger as the Lord. He prepares breakfast for them and they eat together on the beach. Afterwards Jesus has a conversation with Peter, asking him whether he loves him, and commissions him to feed Jesus' sheep. Peter then asks Jesus about the particular vocation of the "beloved disciple." He receives only an enigmatic reply: "If it is my will that he remain until I come, what is that to you? Follow me!" Then the gospel ends with an awkward reference to the innumerable words and deeds of Jesus that the writer could not include in his book.

Close examination shows that this last chapter of John is an appendix added later. John 20:30 was clearly the ending of the first edition of the gospel. It looks as though this last chapter was added to meet a particular faith situation which had crystallized a few years after the gospel had first been issued. Scholars suggest that John's church had always been out of the mainstream, rather self-consciously on the fringe and jealous of its identity. But there came a time when this church needed to reckon with the claims and authority of the other churches deriving from the apostles, especially Peter. So this chapter was written to summon the community in John's tradition to be in unity with the other apostolic churches by showing that Peter's terrible betrayal had been reversed and that he had been restored to leadership by the Risen Lord. The last chapter of John presents a developed version of what must have passed between them, Peter's acceptance of reconciliation after his threefold denial and Christ's empowering gift of trust. So the passage, though not a transcript of the conversation, puts me in touch with the mysterious original encounter between Jesus and Peter.

Peter's original situation is not the same as mine. The situation of John's church in a critical year toward the end of the first century is not mine. But the word which emerged from both of those is charged with a surplus of meaning and power through which God can engage me in my own place, my particular turning point. I find myself being asked by Jesus, "Do you love me?" The answer to that is not thoughts about Peter's situation. I have to give my own answer. The Scripture gives me courage to overcome my hesitations and qualifications. With Peter I may find myself saying what I truly want to say, yet so often stifle: "Yes, Lord, I love you!" (You may just now want to ask yourself when you have said that to Jesus in just those words, with that directness.) Or another time I may find myself having to say for some reason that I do not, and move into a prayer of confession, lament and longing to receive the gift of the energy to love.

Or the words "Feed my sheep" may strike me. I am not an apostle in the way Peter was. But I am asked by the living Christ to feed his own. My response to the words "Feed my sheep" is not some discourse about church leadership. My response is to search my life to discern whom it is that I have the power to nurture and sustain. I am called to be one who feeds others. My prayer will lead me to those whom I tend to starve out, or deprive. Or it will lead me into wonder and thanksgiving that in spite of my own needs and shortcomings I do have gifts and power to nourish the lives of others for whom I bear a responsibility to Christ.

In other times of prayer other words will strike me, for instance the warning of Jesus about Peter's martyrdom. "'Truly, truly, I say to you, when you were young, you girded yourself and walked where you would; but when you are old, you will stretch out your hands, and others will gird you and carry you where you do not wish to go.' (This he said to show by what death he was to glorify God.) And after this he said to him, 'Follow me'" (John 21:18,19). These words are not an oracle about my particular death. But they carry meaning for me, they pose questions from God. They make me ask how I am dealing with the constraints of my life, the way it is not turning out as I want, the losses and contradictions which thwart my dreams and wishes. What have I got to say today to the Lord about the way I am being taken where I do not wish to go? What have I to complain about, ask for,

God Touching Us Through the Scriptures

let go of? And the words bring the prospect of death back into my field of vision from the shadows to which I habitually banish it. No, I won't be crucified upside down in the Coliseum, but I am deeply reluctant to face death however it will take me. Maybe in my prayer today I need to say that, open myself to the meaning that Jesus' resurrection has given to it, hear his words to me, "Follow me."

If you look closely at the whole chapter you might gradually become aware of many other questions that could emerge from the text and stimulate a response in prayer. The disciples have caught nothing, the boat is empty and their night on the lake has been completely wasted. Jesus, still unrecognized, questions them and they are forced to own up to their emptiness. Then they are spurred to action by his recommendations and the result is a magnificent catch of fish. The story can bring us into touch with feelings in our own lives of emptiness and futility and wasted time, with questions of discouragement and perseverance, with issues of trust and openness to Christ's invitation. Peter's restless curiosity about the beloved disciple and his question, "Lord, what about this man?" could put us in touch with the tendency to compare our own path with that of others, to get stuck in envy and jealousy, to want to control others or penetrate their secrets. This part of the Scripture gives Christ an opportunity to bring us back from these strayings and obsessions and focus on our own life with him. And so we could go on finding new themes and possibilities.

In many cases the richness of meaning of certain passages of Scripture has been enhanced in later centuries through the worship, song and spiritual tradition of the Church. The most obvious example is the Song of Solomon or Song of Songs. This book of the Bible is a cycle of erotic poems with no reference to God at all. It may derive from the festivities at funerals through which ancient peoples defied death by celebrating the generative power of sex. It is quite possible to use the Song of Songs in prayer to experience the affirmation of sexuality. But in fact the book has been used from early centuries to celebrate God's passionate love for us, and the bliss and intensity of our responsive desire for union with our Creator. By the high middle ages there were over two hundred commentaries on the Song of Songs which interpreted it mystically in terms of the love affair between God and human beings, God's wooing of us, and the vicissitudes of losing and finding one another. This is so woven into Christian spirituality that we have no sense of doing violence to the text or indulging in unwarranted fantasy if we take some of the verses of the Song of Songs as God's declaration of love to us and use them in prayer. "My beloved speaks and says to me: 'Arise, my love, my fair one, and come away; for lo, the winter is past, the rain is over and gone'" (2:10,11).

Likewise Christians experience many parts of the Old Testament speaking to them of Christ even though the writers were originally referring to figures of their own day. We read in Isaiah words from the passages about "the suffering servant" such as, "Surely he has borne our griefs and carried our sorrows; yet we esteemed him stricken, smitten by God, and afflicted. But he was wounded for our transgressions, he was bruised for our iniquities; upon him was the chastisement that made us whole, and with his stripes we are

God Touching Us Through the Scriptures

healed" (53:4,5). Following a tradition going back to the meditations of Jesus himself we experience him in these words. These words of an unknown prophet, whose writings were combined with the record of Isaiah's ministry, are now saturated with references to Christ, who "emptied himself, taking the form of a servant . . . and became obedient to death, even death on a cross" (Phil. 2:7,8). They now bear down upon us with this massive weight of meaning.

The Bible does not come to us from the past with meanings frozen in place at the time the Scriptures were collected. It has gained in meaning, with each successive generation contributing to the stream of tradition. When we pray with Scripture, God is free to touch us through the medium of the inspired associations and overtones that passages have acquired in later Christian usage.

This theme of God's unrestricted freedom in communicating with us, and the many-layered depths of meaning in Scripture gives us the most helpful approach to the teaching that Scripture is inspired. This doctrine does not mean that the Spirit of God dictated the writing and freeze-dried a single authoritative message into each portion of text which we then must simply accept and apply to our lives, as fundamentalists often seem to hold. Rather the inspiration of Scripture refers to the power of the Spirit to unveil saving truth to us, to let the truth stand out in all its transforming power, through the incredibly rich revelatory network of the Scriptural stories and symbols.

St. Paul strikes this note in his second letter to the Corinthians where he is contrasting the undreamt-of depths of meaning in the Jewish Scriptures that have opened up to

Christians in their prayer and worship since the outpouring of the Spirit, with the limitations of the traditional synagogue removed. "Yes, to this day whenever Moses is read a veil lies over their minds; but when a man turns to the Lord the veil is removed. Now the Lord is the Spirit, and where the Spirit of the Lord is, there is freedom" (3:15-17). The image of the Spirit as the one who strips away the veils concealing reality as we embrace it, so it can embrace us, corresponds to the concept of truth embodied in the Greek word for truth used in the New Testament. *Aletheia* means literally "unhiddenness." Truth happens, so to speak, when concealments are stripped away and reality emerges into openness. The Holy Spirit who breathes and blows through the world of words and images in Scripture, is endlessly versatile in uncovering the judging and healing truth to us through them, setting us free from impotence, denial and ignorance. "Where the Spirit of the Lord is, there is freedom." Truth happens in prayer, in experiences of disclosure which are freeing. "The truth will make you free" (John 8:32).

A common experience in reading is to feel that there is more to be got out of the words before us. Likewise when we read something again that we particularly admire, we often get something new from the text. It isn't that we merely overlooked that something the first time we read it. Rather we sense that something new has happened in our experience since that time which has made us eligible to grasp a nuance which was present all along. These experiences should encourage us to get rid of the idea that words have only one meaning. Words mysteriously embody many levels

God Touching Us Through the Scriptures

and nuances of meaning and they unfold themselves to us in a process which depends on the changes and developments in our life experience. Nowhere is this more profoundly true than in our experience of meditating on Scripture. Over and over again we return to passages and find new meanings in them. The Spirit is showing us new meanings for which we were not ready the first time, and which could only remain hidden until we had absorbed what was disclosed earlier and our lives had undergone some movement.

Beginning to read the Bible seriously is rather like visiting a vast art museum. We are bewildered at first by the profusion of images and tend to survey them all in a daze, pausing before only a few of the most famous or striking works. But if we begin to make regular visits we learn to contemplate just one object at a time and let it work on our imagination. In time a single painting or sculpture can come to show us many things about life. It can work many changes in our understanding and vision if we allow it to. In the same way one scriptural symbol can in time work changes in us at several levels through the power of the Spirit.

Consider one of the central symbols of the Bible: the exodus from Egypt. It recurs again and again in both the Old and New Testaments. At first the symbol may work on us by inviting us to explore in prayer the implications of the historic event itself. The event reveals God as the One who takes up the cause of the defenseless, the exiled and op-pressed. God does not soothe the oppressed with promises of heaven, but wants their freedom in this life. In our medita-tion on the Exodus event we find ourselves challenged: do we really look to God as liberator? Do we hear God saying today to those who hold their fellow human beings in various kinds of political, social and economic bondage, "Let my people go"? Where do we stand with regard to the oppression perpetrated by the powerful of our own day?

The symbol may then have another effect on us. It is used in the New Testament to interpret redemption, the liberation which Christ achieved through the cross. Luke represents Moses and Elijah at the Transfiguration speaking of "the *exodus* which [Jesus] was to accomplish at Jerusalem." In meditation on the theme of redemption we find our hearts searched and tested. What do we believe Christ has done for us? What was the slavery we were powerless to escape from? What did Christ do to set us free? Do we in reality look to him as our liberator and rescuer? As we explore for ourselves what it is we have been emancipated from, what kind of promised land is now ours to enter, our meditation begins to turn into praise of Christ.

Then other facets of the symbol may begin to claim our attention. The Exodus story tells of years of wandering in the wilderness. It exposes the infidelity of the newly liberated slaves who are full of complaints and resentments, lapse into idolatry and look back in nostalgia to the good food and security of Egypt. The desert stories might speak to us of our moral and spiritual struggles as we journey. We are not yet in the promised land. We rebel against the hardships and struggles of pilgrimage. We resent having to keep on moving in life, and hanker for the security of those who have come to terms with their slavery. The stories of wilderness touch us at a moral level, telling us that our conversion is not complete. The symbol leads us to the prayer of confession,

God Touching Us Through the Scriptures

in which we show God that we are aware of our addictions and persistent enslavement to sin and ask for the grace to be set free.

Eventually the Exodus symbol could evoke an even deeper response. The symbol of the Promised Land evokes our longing for a transcendent home, for an ultimate peace in union with God. In prayer we are able to reach out towards a final homecoming to God and acknowledge that no earthly fulfillment we can expect in the years that remain to us before we die can possibly satisfy that transcendent yearning. There is a final Exodus awaiting us, the passing through death into the life to come. And from time to time as our meditations lead into contemplation we will experience foretastes of that union with God.

Meditation on the Scriptures was so much the basis of monastic spirituality in the church that this experience of the power of symbols to affect us at many levels gave rise to a scheme of biblical interpretation which guided prayer for over a thousand years. This teaching of the four senses of Scripture taught people to interpret the biblical stories and images from four different approaches which correspond to the examples I have just given. The first approach is through the literal sense in which we deal with the manifest, historical meaning of the text. The second approach is through the allegorical sense in which the text symbolically points to the person and work of Christ. The third approach is through the moral sense in which we let the text summon us to repent and change the way we live. The fourth approach is through the anagogical sense in which the text elicits from us in contemplation our transcendent desire to be united with

God. This ancient scheme had been almost forgotten outside monasteries until recently, but interest in it is reviving as the practice of scriptural meditation grows.

Finally there is a need to deal with one obstacle which discourages some modern Christians from embarking on the practice of praying with the Scriptures. They are reluctant to protest to God over what they find in a passage and argue in prayer. For example, a woman who has chosen the single life and is keenly aware of the age-old social and political and religious repression of women is not going to get very far into meditating on 1 Timothy before coming across a passage which seems to reinforce this repression: "Let a woman learn in silence with all submissiveness. I permit no women to teach or to have authority over men; she is to keep silent. For Adam was formed first, then Eve; and Adam was not deceived, but the woman was deceived and became a transgressor. Yet woman will be saved through bearing children, if she continues in faith and love and holiness, with modesty" (1 Tim. 2:11-15). What is she to do with a passage like this? Slam the Bible shut in exasperation and disgust, making a mental note to skip over this provocative passage in future?

An alternative is to allow the passage to provoke a response to God. Then she expresses her distress at the clumsy theology and rigidity of this particular biblical writer, and laments the continuing resistance of the church to the entry of women into their full freedom and authority. The Holy Spirit uses the Scriptures to provoke our passion and protest as well as to invite our consent and acceptance. The Scriptures are not a uniform compendium of oracles of equal authority. Woven into the tapestry of magnificently power-

God Touching Us Through the Scriptures

ful witnesses to the will of God which summon our wholehearted assent are some dim and faulty threads which no longer hold, some really inadequate answers to the right questions. The landscape of Scripture has thorny places, where we have to continue in conversation with God and go beyond some of the positions accepted by the earliest Christians. The best response to these difficult places in Scripture is not to censor them but to let them give rise in prayer to our conversation with God. Usually prayer restores a sense of proportion and it can emerge that some of these galling passages are not in fact the places where we are most in conflict with Scripture. More often it is the Beatitudes, to which we pay lip-service, which turn out in fact to be far more painfully strange and disturbing to us, than some of Paul's controversial positions and the occasional lapses of some New Testament writers from the radical freedom of the original gospel.

You can tell that the path recommended in this book is one which some contemporary Christians are following but is scandalous and incomprehensible to fundamentalists because it is open to the critical interpretation of Scripture. On the other hand the practice of praying the Scriptures leads us away from the dry plain where the Bible is there to be mastered intellectually, dissected and fought over in controversy. The path of meditation leads into love of the Scriptures, an acceptance of their converting authority and an absorption of their treasures into our beings which is beyond the imaginations of those who confine themselves to study and argument over the Scriptures.

Chapter Five

6

When And Where

In this chapter our almost exclusive focus is on finding times and the space for the practice of meditative prayer. And we shall consider how we allow our bodies to participate as fully as possible in our praying. It is important to stress from the beginning that meditative prayer is only one of the disciplines that belong to the larger pattern of Christian discipleship and responsible, healthy living. I am presupposing here that you belong to a worshipping community and play your part in the liturgy Sunday by Sunday. I assume that you will continue to pray, even if only briefly, the everyday prayers all Christians offer, asking for God's grace, interceding for others, giving thanks for daily gifts from God and so on. I expect that some will adopt the practice of daily reading of Scripture. Others will be helped by the practice of praying the daily office of the church, reciting in private day by day either or both of the short morning and evening services with their appointed psalms and Scripture passages. This has been a feature of Anglican life with its foundation in the Book of Common Prayer, and Roman Catholic spirituality in the Liturgy of the Hours. It is now being adopted by some Protestants who appreciate the sense of praying with the larger community that this practice cultivates, and the way the office helps us absorb the Scripture into our lives. Some will have a discipline of regular reading, others of keeping a journal. All these practices and many others we could mention are intended to help us maintain our attentiveness to God and nourish our sense of God's presence. They all require discipline.

In what follows we shall concentrate on the single issue of incorporating into our lives a rhythm of meditative prayer. I find the word "rhythm" attractive. For some people the word "discipline" has overtones of unyielding regulation and stern subjection of spontaneity, but rhythm belongs to all organic life. Without rhythm there is no beauty; without rhythm there is chaos. Unless we take responsibility for the patterning of our lives others will dictate to us how to live. In spiritual life we are not striving to subject our lives to a rigid scheme. We are seeking to find those rhythms and patterns which allow each aspect of ourselves to have its rightful place in life and its proper share of our energy. It is absurd to pretend that in the chaos of our secular environments and under the schedules imposed by our work and responsibilities this quest for balance and rhythm can be anything other than a very demanding one.

"When you pray, go into your room and shut the door and pray to your Father who is in secret; and your Father who sees in secret will reward you" (Matt. 6:6). Although it must have been common to pray aloud in public places, Jesus warned his disciples against it. It was dangerous because the audible words of devotion and the demonstrative gestures and movements attracted the attention of others. The insincere could exploit this attention and even when there was no blatant hypocrisy the temptation to act out a role for the benefit of passers-by was insidious. How could one maintain a single-hearted attention to God when one eye was open to monitor the impression produced by one's devotion on those around?

Jesus could have recommended his followers to go on praying in public as before, but to suppress all outward signs of being at prayer. "When you pray, make it appear to those around as though you were merely carrying on your everyday business. Speak to God silently and don't give yourself away by any movement or gesture of worship." This might have appealed to us as subtle and "spiritual" advice. Isn't this, after all, just what many of us try to do? We pray "in our heads" while keeping up the appearance of merely walking the dog or of being lost in the usual reverie of subway passengers. And we are right in thinking that such invisible prayer is necessary for those with no privacy or little leisure, and for everyone learning to pray continually. In the midst of various activities and all sorts of places where other people are around prayer wells up, and we pray then and there rather than store up the inspiration for later. But the fact is Jesus made no such recommendation. Instead he told his followers to secure complete privacy for their prayer. He told them to pray in secret, and this secrecy was quite literal and concrete. It was not a matter of interiority, an inner solitude of soul. It is the privacy of a room with the door shut.

We probably find this instruction rather banal because for privileged western people, having one's own room is something taken for granted. A moment's reflection reminds me that this is a luxury as rare in the ancient world as it is unimaginable for millions of families today who live crowded in tiny dwellings with few rooms. But Jesus' teaching about finding privacy was not an aside meant for the ears of the prosperous only. His insistence on shutting the door of a room was aimed at ordinary people who would have to make a special effort to secure privacy.

What are we to make of this emphasis on praying alone in secret? We must take it as an expression of the supreme value Jesus placed on purity of heart, and having a single eye. These idioms refer to a consistency of purpose, an integrity and whole-heartedness. It is the gift of being wholly present in what we do and are, of giving ourselves entirely to God and the present without being distracted by anxiety for the future or torn by loyalties to human conventions and expectations. Prayer in private is prayer which can give God undivided attention and in which we can be wholly ourselves without the inhibitions imposed by the presence of others. Unobserved and free from the fear of interruption, there is no need to behave as if we were actually engaged in something other than prayer. If we cry the tears may flow without disconcerting others or arousing their curiosity. If we are moved to hold out our arms or fall face forward on the ground we are free to do so without second thoughts. Privacy makes undistracted stillness possible and encourages exuberant expressiveness meant for God's ears and eyes alone.

Yet we who have easier access to privacy than any other culture in history has provided are surprisingly reluctant and sluggish when it comes to ensuring aloneness for prayer. Next to having no time for prayer, the excuse most readily given for not engaging in serious prayer is not having a place suitable for it. Even people who have their own bedrooms are heard complaining that they have nowhere to get down to prayer. Even before prayer can begin there is a mental block which inhibits many people from clearing the space to pray in their own place.

There are at least four factors at work. First, some of us who cannot seem to find the right circumstances to pray in our own homes are reacting from an unconscious resistance to intimacy with God. Deep down we recognize that Christ is inviting us to a depth of prayer in which we can let ourselves go in love for God. To really let go we need to be undisturbed, just as lovers do. As long as anyone can burst in upon us, it will be impossible to let down our guard enough for this intimate prayer to take place. If then I find myself praying with the door ajar, ready to snap the Bible shut and pretend to be finished or to have been doing something else as soon as my husband comes in, it is likely that I do not really want to let go. If I try to meditate surreptitiously over a cup of coffee in the sitting room before the others are up and about, and have one ear cocked to detect signs of my children stirring so that I can hastily get up if they appear, maybe I feel unready for prayer that could draw me into deep awareness of God.

Second, we are revealing the extent to which we are subject to a suspicion of solitude prevalent in our culture. Especially in North America, closed doors can often excite resentment. Shutting the door is often interpreted as stand-offish, even hostile; we suspect that the person who has shut themselves in has intended to shut us out in order to nurse a bad mood or make a statement. A family or household which respects and encourages the desire for periods of undisturbed quiet is nonconformist.

Third, our reluctance to find privacy in our own homes for prayer is rooted in our shyness and lack of candor about our desire to pray. In nine households out of ten there is no real chance of getting time to ourselves in a room without the consent and cooperation of everyone else. Most of us would have to negotiate for periods of quiet time, and in order to make a bid for others to leave us undisturbed and protect our privacy we would have to be quite explicit about what we intended to do and why it is so important to us. Our reluctance to share with others our desire for meditative prayer is partly due to embarrassment about seeming to be unusually "spiritual." But it is also rooted in a cunning desire to avoid accountability. If I tell others that I intend to set aside a couple of times a week for meditative prayer, and work out with them times when it is convenient for me to have a room to myself for prayer, my commitment to prayer is now made public. So if the chosen time comes around and I am not making the move to go into my room and shut the door I am vulnerable to being reminded of my intentions by my companion or family member: "Isn't this the time you said was ideal for your meditation? I was going to watch this TV program, which you said you don't enjoy, during your half-hour." If I don't tell others about my intention to pray and merely hope for the best in improvising periods of privacy no one will know if my motivation withers away and I begin to let meditation lapse.

Chapter Six

Fourth, even if we do have a room to pray in and can shut the door for half an hour without being disturbed, we often find ourselves at a loss to know how to settle down. Our bedroom, for example, is arranged for sleeping, for dressing, for making love. Where do I put myself in order to pray? It is awkward to perch on the side of the bed. If I sit on the stool I find myself looking into the mirror. In this armchair I end up looking at the closet door or into the neighbor's yard . . . and so on. Not knowing where to put ourselves or how to *be* at prayer in our own place contributes to our reluctance to get down to prayer regularly.

In order to build meditative prayer into our lives we need to discover an appropriate discipline of time and place and then secure the support of those we live with.

THE TIME TO PRAY

Take the issue of time. Meditation on Scripture takes a certain length of time, the same way that meals take a certain length of time to prepare and eat. A typical session of meditation would last from half to three-quarters of an hour. It takes some time to settle down and focus, some time to assimilate the Scripture passage, some time to allow ourselves to be touched, some time to express our response, and some time to emerge and resume our activity. Clearly this is not a length of time which most people can devote to prayer everyday. There is not reason why they should. This is a kind of praying which there may be time for only twice a week, or even once. As a person grows to cherish those times and derive their benefit, she may want to make sacrifices in order to secure a third time. But finding the time for one or two sessions of meditative prayer a week is the place to start.

Can you secure one forty-five minute period of prayer in your weekly routine? If it is truly impossible, then God is not inviting you to this kind of prayer; if you are a pregnant mother caring for three children under seven, this is not likely to be the time for establishing a rhythm of meditative prayer. But another woman's discovery that she is incapable of forty minutes of focused solitude in a week is a revealing one. It may be a judgment on her life. She has allowed it to become choked with too much work, too many responsibilities. Her life has become diseased with the chronic affliction of modern urban society. The crowdedness of her routine show that she has succumbed to addiction to activity and distraction, and finding the time to pray may be one of the ways she is meant to make a bid for health. God's call to "do the impossible" by beginning to pray meditatively may be an element in a summons to start overcoming the disease of overcommitment.

Can you secure one or two times for this kind of praying which you can reasonably expect to be available to God with some attentiveness? If we pursue some ideal of praying only when we are fully rested and alert we may never pray. But it is no use setting aside a time for prayer in which one is dog-tired or still half-asleep. It is tempting to relegate prayer to hours left over from our preferred pastimes, when our energies are low and our mind scattered. God is inviting us to experience love and respond from the heart rather than to spend half an hour fighting off the sleep for which our bodies and minds cry out at the end of the day, or from which we have hardly begun to emerge first thing in the morning.

Experiment usually give rise to a personal pattern, as these answers to a questionnaire reveal:

A business man with a family: "I am fortunate enough to be a morning person and to have a den in my home. I get up an hour before the rest of my family, and twice a week, instead of my usual brief prayers and reading, I have a time of meditation with the Bible."

A single woman: "I use my bedroom to pray in and like to pray after I have gone jogging on Saturday. That freshens me up and I feel rested and alert. Earlier in the week I spend one of my lunch hours in a church near my office."

A married woman: "My husband is not very supportive of my spiritual life, to say the least, but I have established the rhythm of going up to the bedroom to pray when he goes out for his Tuesday evening meetings, and insist as well on having the room to myself for prayer later on Saturday afternoon, when I usually pray over Sunday's gospel."

A student: "I take a break for exercise most afternoons and when I get back I put up a Do Not Disturb sign for an hour. People have gotten used to it and I pray after showering. I study until late at night and get up late, so around five p.m. is a kind of mid-point in my day when it feels right to pray."

A married couple: "We haven't much room in our apartment. Our practice is to pray together briefly in the mornings before we go to work. We both try to meditate for half an hour about three times a week, and the present arrangement is to take turns to cook the evening meal. While one is free to pray in our bedroom the other is preparing the meal. It seems to work well. We tried meditating together, but found it kind of inhibiting."

An artist: "I live by the ocean and always pray out of doors except when the ice is thick on the rocks! There are some rocks where I can sit in complete seclusion looking out to sea. I take an old blanket and my Bible. My dog sits quietly a little lower down."

A priest: "My practice of praying with Scripture, which I first experienced on retreat, kept on petering out until I finally raised the issue with the other three members of the parish staff and asked for their help and support. We talked about my need to have at least three good times to get down to meditative prayer in the week. They were the ones who came up with the idea that on Monday, Wednesday and Friday I would not come to the office until 10:00 a.m. I was amazed that they could accept that; I would never have suggested it myself. I have a 'prayer corner' in my study, and go there once my children have gone off to school and my wife has gone to work. I felt guilty about taking the time at first but gradually I am accepting that prayer time is not stolen from my work. It is what being a priest is all about."

Ask yourself whether you are prepared to reveal your desire to secure times of prayer to those you live with and to be explicit about when and where you want to pray. Are you willing to negotiate your privacy and enlist their active support, or at least their consent?

Chapter Six

Are you aware enough of your own body rhythms to imagine when you might be best disposed for this focused, quiet activity of prayer? Are you best after exercise? Do you feel more relaxed after a bath or shower? When are you most frazzled and tense, or drowsy? Finding the right time for the right things is half the art of living. It is good to be aware of what would be ideal, what would be most helpful, even if our work or commitments mean that usually there has to be a compromise and prayer may have to take place at another time.

Now what about the place to pray? It is typical to assume that all that is meant is finding a nice spot to kneel or sit down. But the space for prayer is the space for our *bodies to pray*. Few people have been encouraged to explore what it means to pray as bodies. We may need to dwell on this to open up unthought-of possibilities.

THE BODY AT PRAYER

It is in our relation to our bodies that we feel most acutely the disease and alienation inflicted by our culture. Vast numbers of people act out their separation from and hatred of their bodies by poisoning them with drugs, alcohol, tobacco and overeating. They torture their bodies with stress, and manipulate them with diets and programs of hectic exercise supposed to promote health, but which are often little more than weirdly punitive attempts to force their bodies into artificial conformity with certain stereotypes cynically touted by the media as images of the ideal. The body as enemy plays out its role in a hundred forms of psychosomatic disease and in pervasive sexual disfunction, which humiliates in private society's public obsession with sexual success. To heal this alienation will require an immense conversion of consciousness. In the meantime, for the individual at least, to reach for wholeness in this chaotic environment requires great resources of nonconformity and imagination. This reaching out should be at the very heart of the practice of Christian spirituality.

In recent decades many Christians have been coming to the painful recognition that our spirituality has been deeply infected for a long time by the same alienations that wrack our society, and that defects and distortions in Christian teaching going back for centuries have actually contributed to our estrangement from body, flesh and earth. Before we can do much to participate in the healing of our culture we have a tremendous amount of relearning to do. We have a long way to go before we really grow out of our muddled ambivalence about sexuality, and shake off a puritanical heritage which has exalted thinking and talking and neglected the wisdom and beauty of the body, the power of ritual and movement and expression, the holiness of the senses.

A starting point is to call into question the minimizing of the role of the body in worship which is so typical of recent western Christianity. In many churches the worshippers' only movements are sitting down, standing up, and bending in an awkward crouching or kneeling position in the narrow confines of a pew. Otherwise all is immobility, except when money is collected. Often worshippers conditioned to these habits carry them over into their private prayer. So the automatic posture of prayer even when they are on their own is to perch against the side of a bed in a hunched-over kneeling position, or to sit in a chair bent forward with elbow on knee and one hand pinching the bridge of the nose. You may not yourself be subject to these automatic attitudes, but you are a fortunate and rare person if you have escaped from the pervasive notion that the role of the body is a minimal one, consisting in "just sitting there."

In order to make the transition into a life of regular meditative prayer most of us need to re-imagine completely what prayer is and can be. And the first principle is that prayer is an activity (and a receptivity!) of the whole person. Or, being more true to our present experience of confusion and dividedness, prayer is an activity in which all that we are seeks the *gift* of integration and wholeness from God. Prayer is a primal human activity which is falsified when any dimension of our humanness is left behind. If in our communion with God we thwart and exclude part of ourselves, the neglected side of our person will still be present as a saboteur and protester, preventing prayer from really "taking off" or going deep. If we try to leave behind our mind, as some do who launch into prayer seeking to suspend all thinking so as to hear what God will say, we will find that the mind, suddenly starved, will dredge up all manner of inconsequential garbage to work on, so that our silence and stillness is invaded by constant distractions. If we neglect our hearts, the imaginative depths in the self which respond to symbols and images and empower our life of feeling, by confining our prayer to thinking religious thoughts and intellectualizing about God, prayer remains dry and effortful, an exercise which leaves us unnourished, and unchanged except for the new thoughts we have to add to our collection.

If we do not involve our bodies in prayer, there are several consequences. We may not be able to enter a true, attentive stillness because our posture frustrates it. Slumped casually on a sofa we become drowsy, kneeling in a tense way we are plagued by pins and needles and restlessness. More than that, we remain inhibited in our self-expression. We use body language and gesture all the time to express ourselves to others. If in prayer we shut down all bodily gesture and movement and confine ourselves to a single position we cut in half our power to feel and own and express our devotion, our love and our needs. Let us then consider the part the body can play in prayer under three headings: the body in place; the body in repose; the body in movement.

As we have said before, we can pray anywhere. But if we act on Jesus' recommendation by entering a room and shutting the door behind us we are making our own space for intimacy with God. As bodies in space we don't merely *occupy* space, we create it. We place our bodies in a meaningful way, orienting ourselves in a certain direction, giving ourselves room for the activity we choose. These common expressions are highly revealing. Room is something we *give* ourselves. The question is how do we make a gift to ourselves of room to pray? In fact, given their freedom, our bodies will draw up appropriately. No one is drawn to pray facing a mirror, or a clock, or wedged behind a door. Our bodies will tell us that we need an area, where we can sit, lie down, stand up or kneel, and where there is nothing distracting in our field of vision. Usually they will draw us into a corner where the walls give a sense of enclosure, privacy and security.

How would you give yourself room to pray so that the place attracts you? Many years ago I discovered that I needed to be as generous as possible in giving myself room to pray. My inertia and trouble with prayer means I need to help myself as much as possible. One gift is a rug to pray on. In Islam the prayer rug is a portable prayer space. Wherever it is unrolled and pointed towards Mecca the worshipper feels orientated. In the corner of my room the rug is there invitingly and when I stand on it I know I am in place for prayer. Within my field of vision when I kneel or sit is a small crucifix made in Haiti from scrap metal; for years before it was a Russian icon of the face of Christ. Below this, on the floor, is a candle on a small candlestick. The pointed flame is itself a wonderful image of prayer, it gives the eyes something simple and lovely to rest on. The ritual of lighting the candle inaugurates the time of prayer; and blowing it out is a nicely definite way of signing off from meditation so that I can resume my normal activity. At the beginning of my prayer time I take off my shoes (an important gesture with links to the words spoken to Moses from the burning bush, "the place on which you are standing is holy ground," and one which tells me that I am here to stay and not run off), I light my candle, and step onto the "sacred space" of my rug. My Bible is at hand to one side; I am ready to move into prayer.

When and Where

These helps in creating an inviting space for meditation are gifts to myself. Be generous with yourself and give yourself everything that might help. It is not easy to pray with our whole selves. Why not make a space which really welcomes you to prayer in your own room? As this extract from a letter suggests, it need not be a permanent feature: "I was intrigued by your suggestion of a prayer corner; until I heard about it I had been trying to pray just sitting on the bed. My room is tiny but I have now discovered that it takes only half a minute to create a really nice space. I pull this little armchair away from the corner, I get my prayer rug from under the bed and unroll it. I take the candle out of the drawer, and there you are! Simple!"

Now consider the body in repose. The body prays when it achieves a posture expressive of trust, attentiveness, poise, at ease in the presence of God. Every posture of the body expresses some meaning and intention. The body is eloquent. It communicates our feeling and state through the symbolic language of attitude and gesture. Prayer is frustrated when the body is put into a position which expresses something other than prayer. Lying down on a sofa is a posture expressing nonchalance and readiness for reverie; the attempt to pray in that position is almost futile because it means something completely at odds with our true situation in the presence of the Living God. The body is not at prayer when it sprawls at a desk, or when it is hunched up over the edge of bed. These attitudes do not *mean* loving and attending to the Beloved, the Holy One.

There is a repertoire of postures which do express and enable simple, trusting communion with God. First, there is sitting. "When the day of Pentecost had come, they were all together in one place. And suddenly a sound came from heaven like the rush of a mighty wind, and it filled all the house where they were *sitting*" (Acts 2:1,2). "And she had a sister called Mary, who *sat* at the Lord's feet and listened to his teaching" (Luke 10:39). Sitting can express many attitudes appropriate to prayer such as waiting, and patience. It expresses being at ease in another's company. We sit in the presence of those who do not threaten us. It is the posture of stability and serenity, of being at home. It is a classic posture for meditation.

To sit still, though, to be really in repose, is an art; the art has a number of basic rules. First, if we are sitting in a chair, it needs to be firm and supportive. Poise and wakefulness do not come from sinking into spongy cushions. Second, the seat needs to be low enough to allow our thighs to be parallel to the ground so that we can place our feet comfortably on the floor. Third, as we sit, we need to have our spine reasonably straight (not ramrod stiff) with our head poised. The chair needs to offer the right kind of support for this to happen, and may need a cushion in the small of the back to help. The experience of generations has established that this basic posture with feet on the ground and back straight allows the breathing to become deeper and a clearer, contemplative consciousness to emerge. It is a wonderful discovery to find that one can sit with serenity for half an hour on a chosen stool or chair, hands resting easily on one's knees or palms cupped under one another in the lap, breathing gently.

When and Where

Alternatively we can sit on the floor. Unless we have learnt some yoga postures this usually calls for cushions. There is an ideal cushion, a kind of low hassock, for sitting at prayer, obtainable from shops that supply Eastern meditation materials. We can improvise cushioning very easily in a bedroom by folding a blanket into four and positioning it against a wall. Then we can sit cross-legged on a pillow placed on the blanket, with another pillow between the wall and our backs to give support.

Another posture is kneeling. We kneel to get down to the level of animals or children and eliminate our standing over them or talking down to them. We kneel before other human beings usually only in moments of extreme emotion when we wish to implore forgiveness or a favor, getting down to symbolize our awareness that we have no claims at all and are dependent on their free choice to favor us. Kneeling means dependence, giving up claims. Kneeling has a place in prayer precisely when these attitudes are the ones we want to enter into or express to God. It has drawbacks as a sustained posture for meditative prayer for two reasons. First, that attitude of supplication is far from being the only one appropriate to our relationship to God, and kneeling all the time could impose on our prayer experience too uniform a tone of penitence. Second, kneeling upright without support is uncomfortable to sustain for more than a few minutes, and few people can sit back on their heels while kneeling without getting cramps.

On the other hand there is a posture which combines sitting and kneeling, eliminates cramp and allows the back to be straight and the head poised. This posture requires a low bench, a sort of shelf on legs, called a seiza bench which is placed over the backs of the ankles when one kneels down so that one can sit back on it. (It is easy to make and instructions are provided in the appendix.) This ancient aid is to be found everywhere nowadays where contemplative prayer is pursued, and the posture it allows is wonderfully serene and comfortable. One can sit on a seiza bench literally for hours without discomfort.

Another posture is lying down flat on one's back. This is a posture which expresses defenselessness, surrender, letting-go. It rehearses death and abandons possessions and status. It allows profound relaxation. It is a posture very appropriate at the beginning of some prayer times in order to enter relaxation, and we could adopt it at the end of prayer time to express letting-go and abandonment. It has drawbacks as a sustained or habitual posture for meditation because it can induce sleep or else so intense a feeling of vulnerability that it can give rise to anxiety.

There is the posture of prostration in which we stretch out face down. This posture expresses awe, self-effacement in the presence of mystery which is overwhelming, worship, grief at our unworthiness, adoration. Again, this is a posture we might well be lead to adopt as part of our response in meditation, but it is not suitable as our basic position of attentive prayer because it is too powerful an expression of abjection and is not open enough to other feelings.

Then, very importantly, there is standing. Standing is the classic prayer posture of early Christians, beautifully portrayed in early Christian art in the figure of the "orans," the woman standing with arms upraised. Standing expresses our sense of dignity and worth. "You have made us worthy to stand before you" we say to God in the eucharistic prayer. Standing expresses the sense of health; we use the phrase "back on her feet" to refer to recovery. Standing expresses the gift of "uprightness," the "good standing" we have before God because through the gift of grace we are clothed with the righteousness of Christ. By standing in prayer at the beginning of meditation we feel our way into the sense of our dignity before God. We rise to our feet during our prayer and at its end to express our acceptance of the gift of worthiness. Occasionally we may even stand for the whole prayer time when we have learnt to stand in repose with arms occasionally raised up, or gently cupped at our waist, or resting simply at our sides.

In order to pray meditatively the body needs to participate through meaningful postures of repose. But repose is not immobility. The body has a vocabulary of movement and gesture—body language. We can express ourselves eloquently to God through this language. God understands body language as perfectly as English and Arabic! It is absurd to suppose that the only way we can communicate with God is by forming words. A movement, a gesture can be even more profound and truthful than a sentence.

The supreme advantage of praying in true privacy is that we can give free rein to the body to worship. Experiment with simple movements and gestures. Sign yourself with the cross as you stand, very slowly indeed. Repeat the gesture several times with calm dignity. Don't think, don't talk, just feel your body expressing the mystery that you are identified with the crucified Christ, you are one with him, you intend to take up your cross, you live from his self-giving on the cross. As you cross yourself, the body prays all these things. The body knows them. Raise your arms above your head and spread them so that your body takes on the shape of a chalice waiting to be filled. Don't form words, sense your body praying your openness to being filled by God's grace. Feel the dignity and reality of this attitude of receptivity. Let the feeling enacted by your body *be* prayer. Stand, or kneel, and lift your hands out cupped together. Let your body in absolute simplicity pray your needing what God has to give. No need for words! As you pray for others stretch out your hands, palms down in blessing, or make a gesture of offering.

Cross your hands across your heart and bow low. The body is expressing a reverence for the mystery of God that you might not have become aware of through thought alone.

In meditation we can respond to God's touch and word to us through gesture, and by changing our bodily posture to one that expresses the new intention or feeling that we are experiencing. We can also deliberately adopt a posture expressive of a particular attitude or address to God in order to experience it. The importance of this is that our bodies can experience and express faith before, or better than, our thoughts can. A Russian friend of mine tells of an unbeliever in Russia who came to a priest longing to believe in God even though his mind was completely closed to belief as a result of years of indoctrination in atheism. The priest surprised him by making no attempt to argue the case for God. Instead he told his visitor to make a hundred prostrations a day for a month. Prostrations are deep gestures used in the worship of Orthodox Christians. Making the sign of the cross, the worshipper bows deeply touching the floor, or briefly sinks to the ground; this is repeated in a rhythm of reverence. The atheist followed the counsel and found before long that his body was worshipping the God his mind had not yet accepted. Gradually his mind caught up with the truth his body had already grasped and he asked for baptism with immense joy.

Sometimes our bodies can pray when our minds are clouded and unresponsive. Movements and gestures can express faith and desire when our thoughts "won't play ball." This means that it is especially beneficial to begin prayer with some gesture and body-language. Our minds are often confused and scattered at the beginning of prayer. The fly-wheel of preoccupation and anxiety is still spinning and we may not be able to think ourselves into attentiveness and recollection. Instead of trying to think our thoughts down it is far better to let the body lead with preparatory gestures and movements, focusing on the feelings that accompany them. We might begin by standing, then calmly raising our hands high and spreading them, sensing the openness in our chest area. Then we could let our hands sink very slowly, eventually cupping them in front of the navel. We might simply concentrate on awareness of our breathing as we do this, or very slowly pray a familiar prayer, such as the collect for purity, which Anglicans know from the beginning of the eucharist. In these gestures the body prays its dependence on the Holy Spirit and its awareness of the Spirit's indwelling at the center. Our minds are now disposed for prayer because they were given feelings and movement to attend to and were lead away from the crowded "mental flea-market."

How do you respond to the invitation, "Give yourself room to pray from the heart"? What kind of space would be your gift to yourself for God, space in the rhythm of your day and week, space to occupy where you could be completely yourself with the "Father who sees in secret"?

7

Entering Into The Stories

Of all the means available to God for drawing us into relationship and setting us free through the truth, stories are amongst the most powerful. Mark highlights one of the most distinctive practices of Jesus when he writes, "with many . . . parables he spoke the word to them, as they were able to hear it; he did not speak to them without a parable" (4:33,34). The evangelist does not suggest that Jesus told stories to make it easier for people to accept his message. He maintains that Jesus told stories to make it more difficult! "To you has been given the secret of the kingdom of God, but for those outside everything is in parables; so that they may indeed see but not perceive, and may indeed hear but not understand; lest they should turn again, and be forgiven" (4:11,12).

It is impossible to believe that Jesus was trying to prevent people from understanding him and being reconciled with the Father, so we must take Mark's forceful words to mean that Jesus used parables to provoke a crisis in the faith of the hearer. The use of parables demanded that the listeners enter into the stories, experience them from the inside, give up normal, conventional responses and allow the flow of the narrative to take them into a new, strange insight where they

Chapter Seven

had never been before. If the listeners were determined to resist the revolutionizing of their understanding of God, and to hang on to the compound of prejudices and traditions which was the received wisdom about God's ways with humankind, then they would instinctively hold back from entering Jesus' strange stories. The parables would only baffle them, while giving off the threatening smell of innovation. A story like that of the vineyard owner who paid all his day laborers exactly the same wage no matter whether they had worked all day or just one hour (Matt. 20:1-16) was not one that many people could dare allow themselves to enter. To experience with every fiber of one's being the truth that God is prodigally generous, and embraces all equally without regard to merit, would not only blow apart the conventional view of God but inevitably lead to alarming questions about one's own readiness to give others the love they need rather than the love they have "earned."

The telling of parables was a process of judgment, not a technique for selling Jesus' message. Some hearers who were ready to risk would enter the story and allow it to do its strange work changing their experience of God. Others would hold the story at bay and defend themselves against the possibility of the bomb going off in their hearts. In reaction to Jesus' parables their hearts would grow harder.

Much of the teaching of Jesus which was gathered by the evangelists is in the form of stories. And in turn these stories are woven into a larger story, the story of Jesus' journey which takes him to certain death in Jerusalem. Mark invented the literary forms we now call a gospel, and he decreed its basic shape and plot by devoting a third of his book to the story of the final suffering, crucifixion and resurrection of Jesus. The stories Jesus told are set in the context of the story Jesus enacted. And that story embodies in the most extreme form the same power as the parables to turn human thought upside down. God's Anointed mangled to death by Roman executioners! God's Son rejected, his mission a failure! The Chosen dies shouting, "My God, my God, why hast thou forsaken me?" It is impossible to enter this story and have one's conventional notions of God's power left intact. Mark is one with Paul in holding that salvation depends on one's readiness to enter into it at the cost of surrendering the standard beliefs about God. "For the word of the cross is folly to those who are perishing, but to us who are being saved it is the power of God. . . . Has not God made foolish the wisdom of the world? . . . For Jews demand signs and Greeks seek wisdom, but we preach Christ crucified, a stumbling block to Jews and folly to Gentiles, but to those who are called, both Jews and Greeks, Christ the power of God and the wisdom of God. For the foolishness of God is wiser than men, and the weakness of God is stronger than men" (1 Cor. 1:18-25).

It is in the light of this story, and as a preparation for it, that the stories are told in the gospels about Jesus, as well as the stories told by Jesus. The narratives of healing, of blessing, of conflict; of meals and expeditions, of parties and intimate conversations; stories on mountains, on lakes, in graveyards; Jesus in crowds, with friends, alone in the desert—are all told in the light of the cross. They are transforming stories with the identical power to provoke a radical reshaping of our experience of God, if we enter into them surrendering our defenses. They become stories mediating the presence of the Crucified One who is alive.

The overarching story of the cross and resurrection, within which Jesus' stories and the stories about Jesus come together, in turn gathers in the stories of the Hebrew Scriptures so that they become newly laden with transforming potential. The drama of the early Christians' discovery of the newly revealing power of the old stories in the light of the cross is condensed in Luke's wonderful account of the walk to Emmaus. "And he said to them, 'O foolish men, and slow of heart to believe all that the prophets have spoken! Was it not necessary that the Christ should suffer these things and enter into his glory?' And beginning with Moses and all the prophets, he interpreted to them in all the scriptures the things concerning himself" (24:25-27).

In Christian faith the Story and the stories within it are not illustrations of truths which could be conveyed in another way. There are no philosophical principles which can be distilled from them and the stories then discarded as empty husks. The stories themselves are indispensable sacramental means of encounter with the Word which became flesh. Just as no satisfactory definition of the kingdom of God can be extracted from the parables, no abstract theory of the atonement can be refined from the passion narratives. The personal engagement with the stories can never be superseded or sidestepped by merely subscribing to doctrines supposedly drawn from them.

Stories are the chief way human beings make sense of their experience. Even when life is hard and complex we can survive and maintain our sanity if our experiences can be told as a story with a thread holding the drama together. Even in our sleep, when the circuits of the brain are firing here, there and everywhere, the mind makes a dream story out of all the material that is thrown up in this busy night-work. We are very susceptible to story-telling of every kind because unconsciously we are constantly on the look-out for plots which might give some clue to the meaning of our own lives. Stories are alluring; it takes an effort to maintain a cold, detached, analytic attitude towards them and restrict ourselves to drawing rational conclusions from them. Stories draw us into emotional involvement with them and work on our passions. And if the story is acted, sung, danced as in the theatre the involving power can be so intensified that we feel immediately the emotional transformation and the infusion of meaning into our hearts that it has accomplished.

Drama is the form of story which is especially revealing of the construction of the human person. The astounding capacity of actors to identify with an immense spectrum of human experience, to get inside, to *be* utterly diverse characters is not an incomprehensible freak. It is an intensification of a capacity that belongs to us all. We all have an amazing potential for empathy with other human lives, for entering into them imaginatively, for identifying with them. Actors and the creators of story and drama develop this common potential through art, but there are countless other ways human beings use it from the mimicry of children to the finely-tuned listening of psychotherapists.

Reflections on our ability to get inside the experience of so many other human beings leads us to ponder the richness and complexity of the self. The range of human experience

Chapter Seven

which we see on the grand scale in society and the world is present in miniature, so to speak, within ourselves. My self is not merely the personality I cultivate for public presentation. There are a host of other selves which just as truly belong to the whole me. I may studiously present myself as a peace-loving and affectionate person, but nightmares, fantasies and the periodic welling-up of irrational rage reveal that there is a murderous self, too, with which I must reckon. A mature man thinks there will be nothing to fasting on a dark wintry day in Lent, but he is taken aback by the depression, anguish and sense of abandonment which overwhelm him when he tries it. Within the self there is still, mysteriously, the baby he once was who is thrown into agony and confusion by missing the mother's breast. We can learn to recognize some of this "cast of thousands" as they personify themselves in human and animal guises in dreams. We can come to identify the stresses, tensions and conflicts manifested by our moods and behavior as rising from clashes and power struggles going on in our inner society.

The image of the self as microcosm, world-in-miniature, is found in the myths of many cultures and in ancient philosophy. It was taken up into Christian spirituality early on. Origen, a great theologian and spiritual master of the third century wrote, "You yourself are a little world and contain within yourself the sun, the moon and the other stars." In our own time it has been developed particularly through Jungian psychology, which has encouraged us to view the human journey as one of individuation. This is the process of maturation through which the obscure and excluded elements of the self are brought at last into integration with the rest. James Hillman, a Jungian psychologist and writer of great power and originality, uses an image for this process which is a particularly promising and intriguing one for Christians. In his early book *Insearch* he discusses our need to encounter and embrace within ourselves "a host of shadowy, unpleasant figures and discover an ability to love even the least of these traits," and asks, "How much charity and compassion have we for our own inner weakness and sickness? How far can we build an inner society on the principle of love, allowing a place for everyone?"

The idea of building an inclusive society on the principle of love, allowing a place for everyone, corresponds exactly to the purpose and nature of the Christian community, the church. His definition reminds us of the teaching of Paul in 1 Corinthians and Romans about the church as the Body of Christ in which every believer is an integral organ or limb. Paul speaks of the church as a koinonia, or community of the Holy Spirit, in which separate individuals from societies, nations and classes at variance are being reconciled and woven together by the Spirit into a new humanity, a new creation. He emphasizes the importance in the church of the lowly and the despised people whom God chooses though they are discounted in the world.

It is illuminating and helpful to think of the Holy Spirit making a church-in-miniature out of the many elements, the many persons, the conflicted and various selves we have within us. Grace does not achieve peace and unity in the heart by rejecting and annihilating inner selves. It heals, blesses and brings them into harmony with one another through love. The Spirit brings all of the selves into relationship to Christ, in whom they can come together.

In the spiritual life I am learning to cooperate with the Spirit in this work of building a society on the principle of love within my self. I am working with God as the Spirit achieves a reconciliation within myself which reproduces at a personal level the reconciliation the Spirit is striving to accomplish with the human race as a whole.

The first way I can cooperate is by recognizing the diversity, the conflicts, the tensions, rivalries, polarities, the riches in my own being. And by finding a name and an image for one of the persons who make up the whole me, I can begin to discover how that person belongs, and how it is allowed, or not allowed its rightful place, what it needs and what it can give.

If, for example, I name within myself the "inner child," I have a way of conceptualizing that living, active residue from my infancy which still vibrates with needs and may be the site of enduring pain. Do I shut my inner child up in the dark, or am I prepared to welcome her or him into the light? When a man names within himself "the woman in me," the possibility arises of recognizing how his own male self has excluded, starved, suppressed or shrunk from a feminine aspect of his being essential for fullness of life. How can she be embraced so that passion, sensitivity and feeling can flow into dried up and frozen parts of his life? And what name can I find to give recognition that there is in me a wounded self which is barren and ugly?

As I find more names for the characters who interact within me I begin to understand the power-politics within the community of the self. Maybe I realize how the intellec-

Entering into the Stories

tual self insists on being in charge and condemns the sensual and passionate self to a shadowy existence in the wings, from which it occasionally sends protests through dreams or escapes in outbursts of embarrassing behavior. Or I realize how the dutiful daughter has elbowed aside the artist and drives me to constant overwork and the placating of people in authority in order to feed her craving for approval. How can this one find acceptance and healing and make room for other parts of the whole?

I can cooperate with the Spirit by bringing the various selves I am learning to recognize into my prayer. So at the end of a harried day of fussing and meddling I may acknowledge in prayer that today "the perfectionist," the fearful self who must guarantee approval by getting everything right, seized the reins and rode roughshod over others. I can ask for the grace and healing needed for this side of myself to make room for vulnerability and spontaneity. I can open myself to healing by renewing my faith in the total approval which is already mine by virtue of my union with Christ and thus let go again of behavior driven by craving for approval.

There are many ways in which we can allow this encounter between God and the many persons of our inner community to take place. Meditation with Scripture stories is one of the most powerful of all. As we have said, we have an innate capacity for identifying with characters in stories, even ones who apparently differ from our personalities. When a strong identification is experienced we find ourselves in the story. We are indeed in the story because the character is representing, embodying one of the persons in our inner society. What happens in the story to the character we have identified with can work a corresponding change within us. We have all experienced this. A writer who is jaded and bored by his own incomplete work and dogged by self-doubt goes to a movie which depicts a painter undergoing many trials and setbacks before being able to create his great work. The writer finds himself in tears in the cinema. In a few days the initial emotional response gives way to a sense of reinvigoration and fresh inspiration to write. The journey of the hero through trials to achievement portrayed on the screen become his journey through the power of identification, enabling him to set out again on his own path of creative endeavor.

In praying with the stories of the Scripture we are consciously and purposefully entering into the stories of divine encounter. Now we allow one of the biblical characters to represent and embody some aspect of ourselves. Finding ourselves in the story by identifying ourselves with one of those taking part in the drama we make ourselves vulnerable to a fresh encounter of our own with the Lord. Jacob, Mary, Judas, Peter, the woman with the hemorrhage and hundreds more personify real aspects of our own selves in relation to God. The words and actions of the woman or man in the story give a voice to and act out inner needs and desires and feelings that are present within us but tend to remain latent without some means of evoking expression. Identifying ourselves with the character allows us to express ourselves to God in ways we might normally censor or avoid. And as we experience the way this character is touched, confronted, healed, invited, embraced, we experience the self it represents being touched by the Lord here and now.

Here are two accounts of meditations on the story of Jesus blessing the children as told in Mark 10:13-16: "And they were bringing children to him, that he might touch them; and the disciples rebuked them. But when Jesus saw it he was indignant, and said to them, 'Let the children come to me, do not hinder them; for to such belongs the kingdom of God. Truly, I say to you, whoever does not receive the kingdom of God like a child shall not enter it.' And he took them in his arms and blessed them, laying his hands upon them."

The first meditation is that of a business executive in his forties, a married man with children: "I really did not want to meditate on this passage. The church I used to attend as a teenager had a sentimental stained glass window of the scene—how I used to despise that window! Well, I spent some time after settling down and reading the passage wondering who I felt drawn to 'be' in the scene. Strangely enough, it occurred to me to experience the whole thing as one of the little kids. I began to imagine the scene from about three feet above the ground! Stuff like my mother fussing and getting me ready to see someone special who was visiting the village, joining other mothers and kids. . .I really got into it. Then I was looking up and feeling anxious and upset as these men started shouting at my mother and shoving us away from the edge of the crowd which was hiding Jesus from view. Then I heard this terrific voice over the shouting and gradually the arguments died down and the crowd parted showing Jesus sitting there beckoning us with his arms. When my turn came to climb onto Jesus' knee I felt this feeling I can't remember having before. I just felt incredibly welcomed. Jesus was delighted with me, ruffling my hair, putting his arms around me, smiling . . . that kind of thing. Well, I didn't need the scene anymore. This feeling of being welcomed was the real thing to pray from. I began to ask Jesus why I hadn't felt quite like this before. Gradually I began to feel how deep was the need to feel that Jesus wanted me. I talked to him about how good it felt to experience him as . . . well, cherishing (not a word I use very often). I realized that I tended to make Jesus into a teacher all the time; prayer had to be heavy, adult stuff. I asked him to 'come through to me' some more in this tender way again. . . . All this is kind of surprising to me. I felt this story had gotten behind some of my defenses."

A woman in her early thirties: "I read the story the night before to sleep on it, and I remember thinking before switching out the light that I could easily identify with the women in the scene. But when it came to my prayer time the next morning, I felt—this was a bit scary—like being Jesus in the scene. I've been meditating like this for some time, but I have never dared identify myself with Jesus and experience a story through his eyes and feelings. 'Well, here goes,' I thought. I prayed that the Spirit would let me really experience the gift she had in store for me in this particular prayer time and would help me move into this kind of unknown territory by 'being' Jesus. It was going all right, I felt authoritative as I taught the crowd and then began to feel the attention of the audience wavering as disturbances broke out on the edge of the crowd. When I realized that the disciples were pushing women away and rejecting their children, I was angry! I felt tremendous, burning anger. I continued with the scene and

Entering into the Stories

felt a deep sense of alliance, of mutual understanding between myself-as-Jesus and the women as they brought their
babies and little ones. I didn't need to say much to them as
I let them gather around me. They—we—just knew that the
secret of the kingdom was with them, it wasn't something
that needed explaining.

So much for the scene. . . . I talked with Christ about this
realization I had been given of his deep, deep empathy with
women. I wondered aloud with him whether sometimes in
my thoughts and prayers I tended to treat him as another
man who couldn't be expected to know how I as a woman
feel. There were feelings I kept back from him. After some
time of taking in the encouragement to really sense that Jesus
knows intimately how I feel, the anger gushed back up. Then
it came to me that I was furious about the low priority given
to the Sunday school at the church I have been attending
for the last year. I am angry at the complacency of leaders
who just allow it to go on with so few resources, and how the
handful of helpers are taken for granted. I prayed about this
anger and asked what to do about it. Was the time ripe to
protest and shake things up even though I was relatively new
in the church? My prayer time ended with my realizing I
needed to pray some more about it, but I felt action isn't far
round the corner on this one."

We notice how identifying with one of the actors in the
story enabled both the man and the woman to pray out of
powerful feelings that otherwise might have remained latent
or unrecognized. Entering into the story made them vulnerable to being surprised by Christ.

Chapter Seven

These have been some introductory insights about the dynamics of meditating with stories. Here are some guidelines about the practice of this way of prayer. Suggestions about selecting appropriate stories will be given later.

1   Select a single story before the prayer time itself. Don't confuse yourself by rifling through the Bible in the prayer time, hoping to hit on one that will do. Reading through the passage the night before will often allow your intuition to work on it in readiness.

2   Spend some moments settling down. Use whatever ways you have learnt to center yourself, such as the very slow recitation of a prayer while you let tension go from your body. Adopt the posture you find comfortable.

3   Ask God to touch you through the passage of Scripture you have chosen. Tell God that you desire to be open to the word, the healing, the probing, the consolation, whatever God knows you need at this time.

4   Pick up your Bible and read the passage slowly and carefully several times. Pause between each reading for half a minute or so to allow yourself to notice details. Let questions and insights occur as you notice more with each reading.

Entering into the Stories

5   Place the Bible aside. Now give your power of imagination free rein to bring the scene to life with yourself as a participant. Don't look at it as if it were a movie projected onto a screen. It is happening all around you. Feel absolutely free to smell the scents of seashore and marketplace. Hear the noises, sense the movements. Allow yourself to become whoever you want in the scene. Are you one of the disciples? A bystander able to see everything happen right there on the spot? Are you the sick person? If so, how are you feeling at the beginning of the story?

6   Let the drama slowly unfold. Let whatever happens, happen. Don't control the story. Let yourself feel what happens. Don't step back out by trying to glean lessons from the story. Don't start thinking about applications to your life. Allow yourself to be affected by the words and actions of the story.

7   As your feelings are affected by the event let yourself respond. Often you need to respond by articulating these feelings to Jesus. Tell him how you have been touched. Ask him what the feelings mean. What kind of gift are they? What are you thankful for? What do you want to ask for? Who is God for you just now? How is God inviting you? At other times the best response is to stay with the impression the story has had on you, savoring it and soaking yourself in it, aware of the presence of the Lord.

Chapter Seven

8   When the awareness dies down of itself, or you feel you have replied and responded to God's way of touching you in this particular prayer, bring the meditation to a simple conclusion by reciting a prayer such as the Lord's prayer or by singing a verse of a hymn. It is better to round off the prayer time positively so you can resume your activity, rather than just let prayer peter out into distraction and restlessness.

Putting guidelines in this form runs the risk of making meditation seem like a strictly ordered procedure, with little room for spontaneity, but spiritual directors who hear many different people talking about their prayer know how infinitely varied are the actual experiences of individuals who trust the wisdom of the basic outline. The advantage of numbering the basic steps is that people who find this kind of praying difficult at first can often identify what is blocking them by checking whether they are neglecting one or more of the guidelines which might be particularly important for them. These remarks drawn from letters written to spiritual directors show how people learnt to identify something missing in their early attempts to pray this way.

"I found at first that I couldn't stay in the scene. I kind of drifted in and out of it. It wasn't very real for me and I kept on feeling I would be more comfortable thinking about the scene. (I lead a Bible-study class and I kept on wanting to find things in the story I might use to stimulate the class.) After several tries I looked back at the guidelines to see what I might be missing and noticed that the stuff about using the senses like hearing and smelling had just not registered with

Entering into the Stories

me. I think, to be honest, that I found the suggestion embarrassing and silly. The fact is that when I gave myself permission to do this I was much less distracted, the whole thing gained vividness. I even enjoyed the smelling bit! More recently I have begun to recognize that I have a kind of puritanical attitude about fantasy. This kind of meditation is allowing me to do something I always thought was vaguely wrong. Sometimes now I really feel touched by Christ in my prayer, and by touched I really mean touched!"

Another beginner reported this experience. "Everything went reasonably well except that I kept on having sort of doubts about whether I had just made it all up and the feelings I had were just conjured up. I felt tentative responding to the feelings I had and wondered whether I was supposed to be getting something else out of it. When I reviewed what I was doing, I noticed that after the first attempt I completely omitted to begin by asking God to give me what he knew I needed. Absolutely typical of me to overlook that! I am the kind of guy that feels if anything is going to happen, it's up to me to make it happen, it's my responsibility. Since I realized what I was doing—or not doing—I have made a point of remembering that God is the one who knows what I am ready for and is able to give me what I need. Asking for it means handing over control. Everything always comes back to this business of trusting, doesn't it? Now I'm starting to accept what happens in the prayer time as 'today's gift'. . . . I am getting less inclined to be self-conscious. And I am getting together some gospel passages about faith and trust to meditate on, as I know this is an issue for me."

Chapter Seven

This kind of prayer is often labelled "Ignatian" prayer because St. Ignatius of Loyola, the founder of the Jesuits, used it as one of the most important tools in his *Spiritual Exercises*, a pattern of intense prayer to be used in a prolonged retreat under a spiritual guide. His handling and interpretation of the varieties of experience that occurs using this method of prayer is unsurpassed in psychological and spiritual acumen. Many of his recommendations for retreatants can considerably enhance the regular practice of meditation in everyday life.

For example, after prayer it helps to look back over the prayer time and recall in a dispassionate way what occurred. What did you notice as especially significant? What did you feel? Was there restlessness, reluctance, deadness? Or did you feel attracted to God, imbued with a sense of trust, and peace? What was Christ like to you? Is there something which invites further prayer and attention? If we just get up from our prayer and take up our normal life without a second thought, a lot of the insight and substance of the prayer can melt away from our awareness and slip from our grasp. If we want to know how God is involved with us just now, we need to register the movements of the heart and of our day-to-day religious experience. Our feelings of coldness and listlessness and reluctance in response to a particular episode in Scripture may be priceless evidence of one of the ways we are being on the defensive against God's will. Conversely, our sense of consolation and being in tune with God's will can tell us where we are growing in faith, in love and in hope. Making brief notes of our experience in a log-book of prayer or a journal can be immensely helpful in setting down the

Entering into the Stories

evidence from which we can gain a sense of what God is saying to us at this time of our life. Here is a quotation from a letter from a priest talking about what keeping a "prayer log-book" meant for him.

"Mine goes back a year, and I have to tell you that I was very reluctant to start one, even though I knew in my head that it is supposed to be a good idea. I hate diaries and have never been able to keep a spiritual journal for more than a week. I had to tell myself again and again that this wasn't a journal to be filled with pages of holy thoughts but a brief record, half a page at the most, of what happened in a meditation time. I procrastinated for a month. And part of the reason for that is that I had been experiencing some rather dark and heavy prayer times in which I had just wanted out! I did not want to see these experiences of restlessness and dryness set out on paper, staring me in the face. But I started. I refused to get fancy, and just used a pencil and a cheap exercise book. What dawned on me after a month or two of honest recording is my tendency to write off negative experiences as a dead loss, best forgotten. I had been telling myself that my prayer was heavy because I was tired, that it would be OK again after my vacation, etc. But when I looked at the record of my prayer experiences I began to see that my difficulties were telling me far more than that I was tired, which I knew in any case. Writing things made me more in touch. Instead of vaguely thinking I was restless, I put down that I was bored, and then not just bored, but angry, angry with God. I was shutting down my prayer because I resented what God had landed me with in this parish and in my marriage. I needed to express that resentment and ask very directly for help and healing. Looking back over the notes I can see that I had been trying to pray while avoiding dealing with my anger."

Pausing to recollect the movements of our heart in prayer can alert us to invitations to return to the same meditation. Our prayer life is not like a train journey where we are inexorably moved on to the next station. Sometimes the word God has for us can only unfold if we return to the same passage of Scripture and allow ourselves another opportunity to listen. We can go back to the place where we felt discomfort and struggle, which is often a sign that we are putting up a barrier to prevent God's approach. Going back to that point allows God a fresh opportunity to melt our resistance. Or we might feel attracted to return to the place in the story where we felt a satisfying presence and joy in order to deepen our appreciation of the gift and open ourselves to further enlightenment and grace. Knowing that we can keep returning to the same passage helps us simplify prayer and remove the pressure to gain everything from it at once. A page from a young woman's prayer journal illustrates a beginner's discovery of the value of repetition.

"Saturday 8th. . . . was reading the story of the crucifixion in John and the words 'behold your mother' stood out, so I wondered whether to start praying next week with passages about Mary. It hadn't really occurred to me before. My Protestant hackles go up at the least suspicion of that Madonna business!

Tuesday 11th. Meditated on the Annunciation. I found myself really identifying with Mary's questioning how this was going to happen. Found myself having all sorts of mis-

Entering into the Stories

givings about becoming pregnant and kept on thinking of the heavy responsibility, the sacrifices, the discomfort and so on. Couldn't really get beyond the sense that all this was too much for me and felt flat about the rest of the story.

Friday 14th. Meditated on Mary coming up with her song when she visited Elizabeth. When I was listening to the words about her joy and all generations calling her blessed, I felt a bit sad as I hadn't felt any of that. I felt I must have missed something last Tuesday. I wonder whether I tend to see everything in terms of duty and what it's going to demand of me.

Saturday 15th. Went back to the Annunciation and started by asking to be touched by Mary's joy as well as her questioning. Found myself just repeating with her the word 'yes.' Gradually I realized that I liked saying yes. It is a beautiful word when it kind of emerges from the cloud of obligation. I talked to God about the heaviness I tend to feel around consenting. So much of my life feels like complying with others' expectations. God isn't like that. This saying 'yes' felt different.

Wednesday 20th. I couldn't get into the story of the birth at Bethlehem at all. I just didn't feel pregnant! When I visualized Mary it didn't feel at all like she was expecting a baby in a few days. So I went back again to the Annunciation scene and really heard the words 'You will conceive in your womb and bear a son, and you shall call his name Jesus.' I allowed myself to sense the presence of a new life within me, in my body. I let my attention stay in this place deep inside me and began to name Jesus there, just gently repeating 'Jesus'. It felt new. Just now I am thinking that I very rarely imagine Christ dwelling in me. Usually he is 'out there.'"

Do not be discouraged if first attempts at praying with stories seem awkward and unsatisfactory. It often takes time for some inhibitions to fall away. It helps at first to home in on passages of Scripture which are especially eligible for this kind of meditation. Choose action stories from the ministry of Jesus to start off with. If you have never prayed like this before, you could begin by simply remembering stories from a gospel you like, looking them up and then noting down the references. Then simply allow yourself to be drawn to one of them. Or you could spend some quiet time with a Bible and notebook and by gently reading your favorite gospel. Note down six or seven stories which appeal to you and use them in turn. You could look up the gospel appointed to be read at the eucharist next Sunday and see whether it draws you. You may want to use the Scripture clusters in the second half of the book to find passages with a particular theme. As your familiarity with the Scriptures grows, you may be able to remember passages which speak to certain needs and states. When you are aware of a certain need you can go to the story which speaks to your situation.

8

Taking In The Word

Jesus valued meals so much that his enemies had grounds for slander: "Behold, a glutton and a drunkard!" (Matt. 11:19) His pictures of the kingdom of God portray the great banquet again and again. The gospels show Jesus feasting with the tax-collectors and crooks, dining with inquisitive Pharisees, miraculously feeding immense crowds out in the wilds, producing an outrageous quantity of wine for a wedding feast. The Risen Lord chooses dinner time to appear to the disciples in the upper room and shares their food, joins the couple from Emmaus at supper, and even cooks a fish breakfast for the disciples by the lake. Above all, on the night before his crucifixion, he made a meal into the means of giving his whole self to believers so that he could live in them and they could live in him. "The Lord Jesus on the night when he was betrayed took bread, and when he had given thanks, he broke it, and said, 'This is my body which is for you. Do this in remembrance of me.' In the same way also the cup, after supper, saying, 'This cup is the new covenant in my blood. Do this, as often as you drink it, in remembrance of me'" (I Cor. 11:23-25). "I am the living bread which came down from heaven; if any one eats of this bread, he will live for ever; and the bread which I shall give for the life of the world is my flesh. . . . He who eats my flesh and drinks my blood abides in me, and I in him" (John 6:51,54).

Feeding on Christ, taking Christ into our inmost selves, is not confined to the moment of communion in the eucharist. The sacrament of Christ as food and drink shows that he is our nourishment in every way. Above all our prayer is eucharistic, the means whereby we absorb Christ as nourishment, Christ who is the Word made flesh. It is probably out of concern lest his people fall into the trap of limiting their communion with Christ to the liturgical celebration of the eucharist that the writer of this gospel actually omitted the institution of the eucharist from his account of Jesus' last supper. Instead, he has Christ deliver a long discourse about the absolute necessity of eating his flesh and drinking his blood much earlier in the gospel, in chapter 6. By inserting the theme of feeding on Christ into the context of the teaching ministry of Jesus, the writer gives it the widest possible application. He can associate our taking in of Christ's flesh and blood with our feeding on all his life-giving words. "It is the spirit that gives life, the flesh is of no avail; the words that I have spoken to you are spirit and life" (6:63). Prayer is a meal in which we feed on the risen life of Christ; the Spirit brings to our remembrance all that Christ has said to us, takes what is his and declares it to us, as John teaches in the farewell discourses given at the Last Supper.

Behind this image of feeding on Christ and taking in the nourishment of the life-giving word is an ancient tradition associating word and food. The prophets had visions in which they were given books to eat. God's message had to be taken into their very being. "And he said to me, 'Son of man, eat what is offered to you; eat this scroll, and go, speak to the house of Israel'. . . . Then I ate it; and it was in my mouth as sweet as honey" (Ezek. 3:1-3). Scribes and psalmists who recited God's teaching called it delicious. "How sweet are your words to my taste! They are sweeter than honey to my mouth. . . . I open my mouth and pant; I long for your commandments" (Ps. 119:103,131). "Taste and see that the Lord is good" (Ps. 34:8).

The intimate connection between communicating—communing—and eating is ineradicable because it is rooted in our bodies. We use our mouth and tongue and throat to speak and we use them to taste and chew and swallow our nourishment. For the ancients the connection was more vivid because even solitary reading was done aloud and the activity of the tongue and mouth was like eating. We use the word ruminate to mean inner pondering. Our ancestors would have been more conscious of literally chewing the words over as cows vigorously and rhythmically chew their cud.

The association between meditation and eating derives from the palate and the sense of taste. The tongue is the organ of discrimination. Faced with an array of liquids and solids we have few clues whether they are suitable or deadly to take into our bodies, beyond the rough signals of attraction or revulsion picked up through the nose. We have to put a trace in our mouths to find out. The fantastic subtlety of the tongue in distinguishing thousands of different tastes is the physical analogue of the power of the human mind to sort out what is good for us, and to discern and identify just what we are being given.

There is a very ancient form of meditation on Scripture for which tasting and eating and digesting is the most obvious metaphor. It stems from the way our predecessors read and was especially cultivated in the monasteries. Its old title in Latin is "lectio divina, "which means holy reading. This way of prayer consists in reading very slowly through a passage until a particular word or phrase "lights up" and attracts the reader. The text is then laid aside and the phrase is repeated in the heart. The one praying simply repeats the phrase, allowing it to unfold without any analysis. When the phrase has been deeply absorbed, it is time for responding to God by expressing the feelings the words have evoked, the needs, desires, the appreciation or praise, in the simplest possible way. If words seem to sink away, then the prayer consists in staying still in the awareness the meditation has fostered, being in and with God. Then when distractions bring this state of awareness to an end the meditation is brought to a conclusion or, if more time is available, the reading can be gently resumed.

Whereas the meditation method outlined in the last chapter is exclusively meant for use with stories, this kind of meditation can be used for every kind of writing in Scripture: psalms, prophecy, letters as well as narratives. Indeed it is meant to be used for meditating non-biblical writings suitable for stimulating prayer and feeding the heart. It is the way monks and nuns have always fed on the writings of the saints, theologians and mystics.

Its simplicity is a little deceptive. It is simple, but it has the kind of simplicity modern women and men can find very difficult to make their own. In the ancient world books were rare and precious. It was natural to read slowly in an almost ritual way. In our world we are bombarded with printed material and information, far more than we can dream of absorbing. We screen out almost all of it and become adept at skimming through pages of text to pick up the bits and pieces we want to use. Our reading habits are completely at odds with the slow, receptive quality of "holy reading." Consumer culture favors rapid reading and fast food. Holy reading is going to take patient practice.

The other aspect of the simplicity of this form of meditation is its use of repetition, rather than discursive reasoning. Many of us have a prejudice which insists that the way to apprehend meaning is to dissect and analyze an expression. We react with incredulity at the notion that simply sounding the words in our hearts as one would gently sound a bell over and over again can be of any use. What passes for education in a culture dominated by technology tends to wither our appreciation for the sensitivity of human intuition and our spiritual capacity to resonate with meaning-packed symbols. A mistrust for something so simple as repetition is unfortunately reinforced in some circles by a phrase left over from the King James Bible. This translation had Jesus in the Sermon on the Mount warning against "vain repetitions" in prayer. It is a bad translation. The practice Jesus was attacking as typically pagan was not repetition, but the heaping up of semi-magical formulas.

Here is a set of guidelines for holy reading. At first it is advisable to pray with texts you have at least some familiarity with. If you try holy reading with a part of Scripture that is completely strange to you, your curiosity may be aroused and it will be very tempting to race ahead to see what comes next. The meditation is not intended to introduce you to something new. It is meant to allow you to *experience* and feed on what you know. Regular reading of the Bible extends the *breadth* of our familiarity with Scripture. In 'holy reading' we absorb the Word in *depth*.

1 Spend a few minutes settling down and pray that your heart may be opened and receptive to the gift God knows you need today. Only the Breath, the Spirit of God, can bring the word to life. Let your own breathing become more deep-seated, gentler, from lower down, as you invite the Spirit to pray in you afresh.

2 Begin reading at the place you have previously chosen, and read on very slowly indeed with an open mind. Don't study the text, just read it slowly, aloud if you find that helpful. This is the "lectio," or reading.

3 When a particular sentence or phrase or single word "lights up" or "rings a bell," seems striking or inviting, put the Bible down. Resist the temptation to go on, and do not start thinking up reasons why the phrase has claimed your attention. Here the reading stops and the "meditatio" begins, the absorption through repetition. So, for example, you might be reading the tenth chapter of John's gospel

Taking In the Word

where Jesus describes himself as the Good Shepherd. As you come to verse 14 these words seem to have a special allure, "I know my own, and my own know me." This is the verse you now meditate with.

4 Gently repeat this phrase or word again and again within the heart. Don't project them outward. Let the repetition be gentle and not mechanical. There is no need to conjure up any mental picture to accompany the words or to try to make yourself feel any particular emotion as you speak them. Resist the temptation to force particular lessons or meanings from the words. You know what the words mean well enough; the repetition is to allow you to savor and relish them at an intuitive level. After some time you may find that a longer sentence or phrase has shortened itself to a single word. Gradually allow yourself to be absorbed in the word. So, "Peace be with you. As the Father sent me, so I send you," might become distilled into the single word "peace" (John 20:21).

In time you will become aware of an impression that the words have made on you. They have evoked a particular feeling or attitude. When you have become aware of this there is no need to prolong the repetition. Now is the time for "oratio," the praying of your response.

5 Express to God in the simplest way the impression the words have made on you. You may want to thank God for the gift they convey, ask the questions they have stirred in you, put into words the longings or needs they have brought up. Keep it simple, praying spontaneously. Or you may want to respond by remaining in loving silence in the presence of God, appreciating the grace or attitude the word of Scripture has instilled. Your prayer may move into contemplation, a simple being in Christ with God in which all you are aware of is that you are being attracted towards God like the needle of a compass finding the north.

6   After some time you will not be able to sustain your spontaneous praying or state of loving awareness. Distractions set in. You may bring the prayer time to a close with thanksgiving or by reciting the Lord's Prayer. If you have time and opportunity, you may feel drawn to begin the process again by returning to the Scripture. Begin at the point where you left off and continue with the reading expecting to be touched again by another word.

A word about repeating the phrase. There should be nothing artificial and mechanically regular about it. The words of an Orthodox monk teaching about the "Jesus prayer," in which the name of Jesus is repeated many times, are helpful. The repetition "may be likened to the beating of wings by which a bird rises into the air. It must never be labored and forced, or hurried, or in the nature of a flapping. It must be gentle, easy and—let us give to this word its deepest meaning—graceful. When the bird has reached the desired height it glides in its flight, and only beats its wings

Taking In the Word

from time to time in order to stay in the air.... The repetition will only be resumed when other thoughts threaten to crowd out the thought of Jesus. Then the invocation will start again in order to gain fresh impetus." ("On the Invocation of the Name of Jesus" by a monk of the Eastern Church)

This way of praying helps us permeate the rest of our day with God's word to us. We can call the phrase to mind at odd moments of waiting or interludes in our routine. Centuries ago men and women carried small bunches of fragrant flowers and would raise them to their noses whenever they wanted to savor the perfume or when the atmosphere was foul. Spiritual writers likened the practice of recalling the word from one's prayer time to this habit. Again and again we can breathe in what the Spirit gave us in the word. In our log-book of prayer we can record which verse of Scripture came to us as God's word on a particular day. The sentence can be written out on a card and placed in our bag or on our desk or bench so that our occasional glances at it revive the impression made on us in the meditation time.

Over time particular phrases of Scripture can become saturated with significance for us. Lovers and friends often acquire a kind of private language or code assembled from expressions, snatches of songs, words from the time of courtship or shared experiences, which have a unique significance for them. Using them in letters and conversations keeps on renewing the bond of love. Praying the Scriptures in the way we are describing builds up this personal language of intimacy with God. When we read the passage again, or hear it in church, certain words and phrases now come alive to us and rekindle the connection with God we experienced

Chapter Eight

when we prayed them.

Here are some reports by a variety of men and women of their experience of this "holy reading" which might help you grasp what this is all about.

The first illustrates how utterly simple this kind of praying can be. It comes from a woman in her sixties who recently joined a group exploring meditative prayer at her church:

"I have always loved the psalms since I was a girl. I like the old translation I am used to from the old Book of Common Prayer. The other morning I looked up Psalm 84 because I like that verse about 'those who go through the vale of misery use it for a well.' But as I read through it slowly I realized that it was the very first verse which seemed to draw me, 'How lovely is thy dwelling-place, O Lord of Hosts.' I just repeated the phrase very softly for some time and I suppose I vaguely had in mind the old parish church I was married in and went to for so many years. But as I kept on repeating the words it gradually dawned on me, taking me unawares as it were, that God dwells in *me*. I am God's dwelling-place, we all are, as Christians, aren't we?

As I said the words some more, I seemed to hear them telling me I was lovely as God's dwelling place! I felt as if I could cry a bit, I don't know how long it has been since anyone called me lovely in any connection, certainly not much since my husband died. I asked God whether it was all right to take these words as applying to me. Somehow I felt God was telling me that he is at home with me, and likes it! What a strange feeling! Actually I let myself change the words to 'How lovely is *my* dwelling-place,' as if God were saying them for a few moments. It is so often I feel rather

Taking In the Word

stupid and unattractive. I have never imagined God *admiring* me before. Later on I felt a bit embarrassed about the prayer, and then I said to myself, 'Why not? Why should we picture God as always complaining?'"

Her prayer is very simple and natural, but we can observe in her description the unfolding of the process set out in the guidelines. She turns to a psalm she already knows. She reads it with an openness of spirit which allows her to sense an attraction not towards her favorite verse this time, but to the opening verse which had never struck her before. She repeats the verse long enough for familiar associations to give way to a new, fresh impression. She allows herself to be moved by the words in their new significance and is open to grace, the experience of God's sheer gift. She is free to allow the words to have an even more gracious impact as she hears them as God's word to her.

Here is another account, this time from the journal of a woman in her thirties. A friend had recommended that she pray with the first part of Isaiah 43, as she herself had found it moving.

"I couldn't recall ever having heard of this passage before and as I glanced through it after she phoned in the morning I could see why Alison treasured it. The words 'You are precious in my eyes, and honored, and I love you' danced out on the page. But I remembered how susceptible I am to trying to experience what other people experience, instead of what is really my life and my feelings, so I started my own prayer time that evening really handing it all over to God and asking to be touched as I needed to be touched. Taking it very slowly, I came to the verse, 'When you walk through fire you shall not be burned, and the flame shall not consume you.' I stopped there. I didn't feel anything very strongly at first, but it is vivid and I began to repeat it. At first it seemed vaguely reassuring and it went on like this for about five minutes, I suppose. Then without warning I reacted. I just wanted to protest 'But I have been burned! I really have!' I had to stop repeating the verse and express the rage that had welled up—again!—about being abused by my uncle as a child. I am so sick of having to deal with it in myself. And where was Christ in all that! That's what I kept on asking. I haven't let rip like that in prayer for a long time, not since the whole mess came up two years ago. 'The flame shall not consume you!' I actually felt I was being sarcastic with Christ as I said these words! As the storm died down a bit the words came back to me again only now they sounded very different. 'The flame shall not consume you.' I seemed to hear Christ telling me that the *flame of my anger* will not consume me. I am so afraid it will. I need to hear that so badly. I told him that. I asked for the gift of believing that I could be angry, work through my anger, my 'burnedness' and that it wouldn't consume me, that healing will come. I am writing this now after talking to Alison on the phone. She was amazed to hear how different the effect on me was from the one she had in the back of her mind when she suggested the passage."

Here is a report given by a middle-aged male priest.

"I have been slipping into my old tendency to pray only about the parish, and people in my care with problems, and I found myself feeling heavy and sluggish in my prayer time. So I have returned to praying with the Gospel of John to get out of the rut. I'm not taking passages in any particular order.

Taking In the Word

I started with the 'High Priestly prayer' in chapter 17 because it was near to the anniversary of my ordination. The phrase which struck me this time is near the end. 'Father, I want those you have given me to be with me where I am. . . .' I repeated it over and over again and the longer I prayed it the more it seemed to me that I had never really heard it before. It sounded very new, very strange. It took me some time to accept that *I* have been given by the Father to Jesus. I am a gift to him! I began to pray about this. I thanked God for giving me to Jesus. I praised him for the security the words promised as I remembered something from earlier in the gospel, 'Now the will of him who sent me is that I should lose nothing of all that he has given me, and that I should raise it up on the last day.' I kind of 'tried the idea on for size' of me being a present. It's not how I usually think of myself, to say the least.

Then I returned to the verse and this time the second half spoke to me. I just repeated, 'Be with me where I am.' It seemed like an invitation to me coming from Christ. Most of my attempts to pray in the last few months have insisted that Christ come down to be where I am, locked into all my responsibilities. This is different. It felt okay to 'lift up my heart' and put myself with him. I just stayed with the sense that there is room for me too to be 'in the bosom of the Father,' as it says in John 1, standing in the stream of all the loving that Christ gets. This is what really stayed with me for a couple of weeks afterwards. I found myself saying in odd moments the words of invitation: 'Be with me where I am.'"

Chapter Eight

This is an account by a single man, an engineer in his twenties who has been baptized only a few years.

"You know the trouble I have had suspecting that meditation is always escapist. But if it's really God you're making yourself vulnerable to, then you'd better expect to be goaded to action. I have had an ironic experience recently, by which I mean that I, who am so eloquent about social action, was 'found out' in prayer to have my own share of inertia. . . . I have been praying with Paul's letters, my early prejudice against him now having given way to a liking for his feistiness. I was reading 2 Corinthians 6 and came to a halt at the phrase, 'as poor, yet making many rich.' So I prayed it as you taught me, reciting it, turning it over. Several times I got derailed by starting to philosophize about the paradox and had to return to the simple repetition. After about ten minutes or so, the words seemed to have really gotten to me and I started to talk to God about how I hated to think of myself as poor. I talk a lot about the needs of the poor—by which I mean, other people, the homeless, not me. As I did this I realized that I think of myself not as poor but rather as having nothing to spare, certainly not enough to make any one else rich. The poor make others rich, but a tightwad can't! It is as if God was really uncovering the mean streak in me, by which I hold on to my time and my energy as a possession. I asked God to show me how I could make anyone rich.

I had no sooner said this when I remembered they were appealing at church for volunteers for a team to visit in a local nursing home. This was a bit painful. I have an aversion to extreme old age. This was tough to pray about. I do feel

Taking In the Word

helpless (poor?) when it comes to the old. What can I say, what have I to offer in this kind of dead-end world, as it seems to me? I didn't feel cornered by God exactly, but I certainly had to do some surrendering. Well, you can guess the rest. I have fancy ideas about paradoxes but by the end of my prayer time I knew that the only way to grasp this one was to act on it. I have signed up for the team. I'll let you know what happens. . . . Meanwhile this phrase of Paul's has gotten under my skin. It keeps on coming back to me and making me think that it might be the key to just about everything in Christianity."

Perseverance in this way of prayer leads to an ever increasing awareness of the power of simplicity in prayer. We experience the way that a few words can say almost everything. It is the sign of burgeoning intimacy when we realize that God can communicate intense love, and profound truth, and depth upon depth of grace through a single word, or just a sentence, and that sometimes all we want to express to God can be communicated in a phrase. In contemplative prayer we trust this simplicity, allowing our hearts to say all that needs to be said, or hear all that needs to be heard in a single phrase, centering ourselves in God and keeping ourselves present to God through the rhythm of repetition. If you practice "holy reading" you can expect sooner or later to be attracted to the kind of praying in which you simply recall one of the words which was the means of grace in a meditation, and resume the repetition of it, letting it be the expression of your desire, your praise, your love, or taking it in as the expression of God's love for you.

Chapter Eight

"I prayed with Scripture several times a week during the two years I wasn't working," a woman shared in a spiritual development group, "and it became a kind of struggle. I felt I ought to be making myself find new passages to pray with. I remember reading somewhere, 'Beware of *oughts* in prayer,' and I think I know what the writer meant. Deep down I was more attracted to going back to some of the single verses of Scripture which made such an impression on me, and staying with them. 'Fear not, it is I.' 'Behold the Lamb of God!' 'With you is the well of life, and in your light we see light.' 'Maranatha! Our Lord, come!' 'Abide in me, and I in you.' 'His banner over me is love.' 'In him it is always Yes.' When I pray these phrases, I don't need to go into the whole Scripture passage. Everything is contained in the phrase, or just one word of it. These days I tend to use a particular word for as many prayer sessions as I want. When it palls I can go to another one I know, or return to the Scripture for a fresh start. This sounds a bit trite, but the thing which helped me do this was that famous line from the Shaker hymn, ''Tis the gift to be simple, 'tis the gift to be free.' This simple kind of centering prayer is a gift of God, and there is a freedom in not having to produce something new in prayer all the time."

There are some parts of the Bible which are particularly promising for initial forays into "holy reading," such as John 13-17; Ephesians; Philippians; 1 John; Romans 5-8; the Psalms; Isaiah 40-66.

9

Gazing

"Taste and see that the Lord is good," invites the psalmist. The last chapter described the kind of prayer most closely corresponding to tasting, eating, digesting. Now we consider the form of prayer which is most like seeing, looking, gazing. The Scriptures give us hundreds of stories in which to get involved, hundreds of "words of life" to assimilate and feed on—and hundreds of images to gaze on, through which the light of God can shine into our inmost selves.

What we see affects us profoundly. The advertisers know this and exactly how best to seduce and manipulate us with images. Artists know it and offer us images which can kindle our souls and liberate us from spiritual inertia if we consent to really expose our hearts to them. With the life-enhancing images of art, as with the beauties of the world, fleeting glances and the momentary attention of preoccupied minds are not enough. We have to open ourselves through contemplative gazing on the image, surrendering our prejudices, letting it be itself, allowing it to disclose the meaning it embodies on its own terms. The difficulty we often have in simply looking at a painting, for example, is a testimony not only to the grip our preoccupations and anxieties have upon us, but also to our fear of being changed. It is as if we know deep down only too well that contemplation is transforming. I often think in this connection of a passage in a letter written by the German poet Rainer Maria Rilke in 1907 to his wife Clara, who was a sculptor. "Gazing is such a wonderful thing, about which we know little; in gazing we are turned completely outward, but just when we are so most, things seem to go on within us, which have been waiting longingly for the moment when they should be unobserved." And at the end of his famous poem contemplating the torso of an ancient statue of Apollo, the poet addresses himself, "There is no part that does not see you. You must change your life." This strange shift, in which it seems as though the work of art is looking at us searchingly, rather than we looking at it, and that it is inviting us to change, is one which all lovers of art will recognize from their experience.

We should not be surprised then that Scripture teaches the intimate connection between contemplation and conversion. John writes in his first letter, "Beloved, we are God's children now; it does not yet appear what we shall be, but we know that when he appears we shall be like him, for we shall see him as he is" (3.2). The experience of seeing God face to face will transform us utterly; we shall come to be like God ourselves. In the background of this doctrine is the profound conviction expressed through the Hebrew Scriptures that no one could see God and remain unchanged, no one could see God and live. The holiness of God is so intense that human beings could not survive direct exposure to the divine presence. Those who were allowed special encounters with God did so indirectly through the mediation of "the angel of the Lord," or were given special protection as when

Moses was told to hide in the cleft of the rock. "I will cover you with my hand until I have passed by; then I will take away my hand, and you shall see my back; but my face shall not be seen" (Ex. 33:22,23).

The early Christian believers still affirmed the impossibility of the vision of God in this life: "No one has ever seen God." But they were witnesses of a radical change in the accessibility of God to human beings. God's Word became flesh in Jesus. Jesus is the new visibility of God: "the only Son, who is in the bosom of the Father, he has made him known" (John 1:18). "The Word became flesh and dwelt among us, full of grace and truth; we have beheld his glory, glory as of the only Son from the Father" (1:14). "If you had known me, you would have known my Father also; henceforth you know him and have seen him. . . . He who has seen me has seen the Father" (John 14:7,9). By faith we can see God by looking at Jesus. But we cannot do so and stay the same. Seeing God in Jesus still means death, but it is our deadness that dies as we look at him, and our true selves that come to life.

Paul expresses the converting power of our contemplation of Jesus in unforgettable words: "And we all, with unveiled face, beholding the glory of the Lord, are being changed into his likeness from one degree of glory to another; for this comes from the Lord who is the Spirit. . . . For it is the God who said, 'Let light shine out of darkness,' who has shone in our hearts to give the light of the knowledge of the glory of God in the face of Christ" (2 Cor. 3:18; 4:6). It goes without saying that the New Testament writers are not referring to a literal seeing. "Without having seen him you love him;

though you do not now see him you believe in him and rejoice with unutterable and exalted joy" (1 Pet. 1:8). The light of Christ shines *in our hearts* through the images of Christ handed on to us in Scripture. We behold his face through the medium of our imagination, an imagination which is not given over to unbridled fantasies of our own, but one which is disciplined to represent in our hearts the living images and symbols which God has chosen as the alphabet, the palette of colors, of revelation.

You will very probably discover the prayer of gazing naturally as you grow in experience of praying with Scripture passages. As you meditate on a story you will find that a particular image or scene absorbs your attention and all the other elements in the story fade away from your awareness. You feel drawn simply to look and remain in an attitude of wonder, fascination or simple attention. There is no desire to converse with God at any length and no sense of needing to make anything happen. You simply feel that you are being impregnated with the image, that it is being taken into your heart, where, just as a photographic negative is later developed into a positive image in the dark room, its mean-ing will disclose itself in God's good time.

This common experience of contemplative prayer with images happening to people who are not necessarily expect-ing it is found in these typical accounts condensed from conversations.

The first is from a woman: "I read the passage in John's gospel where Christ appears to his disciples in the upper room the evening after his resurrection. I tried to picture the scene but quite honestly found it too much. I didn't really know how to imagine Christ appearing. What happened was that I seemed to come to rest on the words, 'He showed them his hands and his side. Then his disciples were glad.' I just 'saw' his hands. You know, for the rest of the prayer time that is all I did. All I was aware of were these hands held out to me. I felt simply shocked by the wounds, I looked at all the lines. I turned his hands over. I can't really tell you what I felt. All that those hands had done . . . I just felt, 'It's all there, isn't it?' What was I doing? Just being grateful, really. You know since this prayer time, his hands keep coming back to me, and I feel moved again, if only for a moment."

This is an account from a man in his late forties: "I've been reading through John because I don't know it very well, and my rector says, 'You can't sip the Bible like wine until you have drunk it like beer!' There was this business in chapter 4 with Jesus and a Samaritan woman, and him saying things like, 'Whoever drinks of the water I shall give him will become in him a spring of water welling up to eternal life.' It didn't do anything for me. Well, I had time on my hands, which is rare for me, and I asked myself why this didn't grab me in any way. It occurred to me that I had lived and worked in cities for thirty years and hadn't seen a spring of water since God knows when.

Gradually it came back to me that when I was a kid I used to mess about in a field near my home where there was a spring. I used to try to block it up with sods but they soon washed away. It never froze in the winter. I thought I really needed to remember what springs are like if Jesus' words were going to get through to me. So I prayed that he would show me what this spring meant. I really imagined the spring I used to play with. I listened to it. I drank from it. I splashed in it and watched it come clear again in no time. When the spring had become real, I imagined it inside me instead of outside me. It had never occurred to me to do anything like this before! I really felt that spring welling up in me. I bet I spent ten minutes just getting used to this sense of something wonderful flowing deep down inside. Then I guess I talked to Jesus about whether it was true that he had given me 'a spring of water welling up to eternal life' that never stopped, or froze over, and that I couldn't foul up."

A woman in her early thirties writes: "You may find this hard to believe but this was the first Christmas I have really wanted to pray about Jesus' birth. It is yet another sign that I am on my way to recovery as the child of alcoholic parents. For years Christmas was unbelievably depressing, confusing, overwhelming and loaded with terrible memories. I just wanted to escape and I just sat Christmas out as far as worship and church was concerned. Lent used to come as a relief!

I prayed the story of the shepherds coming and finding Mary and Joseph and 'the babe lying in the manger.' It sounds so simple but all I wanted to do was kneel and look over into the manger. That's all, just look at the baby. Time sort of stood still. There was no need to do anything complicated. My mind wandered now and then, but all I needed to do was go back to where I was, just in a kind of still state where I felt, but did not have to say—don't laugh at this, I know it is the famous line from 'Casablanca'—'Here's looking at you.' It is impossible to describe what an experience like this means to me. To feel that no demands are being made on me, to feel absolutely safe in Jesus' presence and actually to

Gazing

be free to adore him—all this is absolutely new to me. I am allowing myself to pray in this simple way a lot now. Do you realize what it means for a person with my background to be allowed simply to *be* who I am with God?"

Contemplative prayer is more common than is often realized. Many people are praying contemplatively though they do not know it. For example, in the widespread devotion of the rosary people meditate on a series of key events in the life of Mary and Jesus, allowing their attention to focus on each "mystery" in turn while repeating the Hail Mary, the Gloria and the Lord's Prayer in a set pattern regulated by the sequence of the beads. The repeated prayers are intended to occupy the mind and keep distractions away so that we can be free to soak ourselves in the grace and meaning with which the great images are saturated. Far from being a technique or the privilege of the spiritually advanced, simple forms of contemplative prayer are the 'bread and butter' of the spiritual lives of millions.

If you feel drawn to contemplative prayer with the images of Scripture, there are two main avenues for beginners to pursue. The first is to consider the elemental symbols which are the basic vocabulary of God's self-disclosure. Light, clay, oil, bread, wine, wind, cloud, robe, fire, crown, tree, river, fruit, yeast, all these words lead us to hundreds of passages where God's being and activity are disclosed through metaphor. For many of us their impact is weakened because modern life insulates us from contact with the natural things used in Scripture as symbols. Only a few people handle yeast and make bread and light fires and lamps. The city's glare blots out the star-filled skies, and awareness of the ancient

Chapter Nine

symbols is smothered by the abundance of new toys and machines. But in spite of the artificiality and hectic over-stimulation in modern existence, deep down our psyches retain an inbuilt aptitude for responding to the ancient, archetypal symbols. Prayer is a way of allowing this deep responsiveness to be brought into play by the Holy Spirit so that the symbols can come alive for us, resonate and connect.

Suppose I open the book of Acts to pray with the passage about the coming of the Spirit on the feast of Pentecost. There are many approaches I could use, but one focuses on the image of the descent of the tongues of fire. Maybe I just never handle fire these days, and hardly ever see it, so that my feelings about fire and my responsiveness to the image are mute and stale, and it will be tempting to start thinking and analyzing instead of experiencing. I need to let fire make itself known to me if God is to touch me in this story.

So in the prayer time I could begin by imagining fire before me, perhaps helped by having a lighted candle in my field of vision. In my imagination I feel and admire its heat and brightness. Then praying to the Holy Spirit, I allow the flame in my imagination to rest on me, as it rested on the first followers in the upper room. I let my awareness flow to the crown of my head, and see with the eyes of faith fire crowning me. I notice any stiffness in me, expressive of reluctance, and relax, really welcoming the fire. Later I could allow my awareness to be drawn downwards from the crown of my head to my heart where the Spirit is now in me. There I worship the Spirit silently and lovingly. I bring the meditation to a close by singing softly the first verse of the hymn "Come down, O Love divine" which expresses perfectly in

Gazing

words what I have celebrated in the prayer time.

The radical simplicity of this kind of praying and the very small part that words have to play often unnerve beginners who wonder if anything really significant is going on. We need to put our faith in God, who works changes in us at a level deeper than consciousness. If we tried to get in on the act and observe the transformation, it would be like switching on the light in the dark room when a film is being developed. If we reflect a little, we can guess at some of the effects a meditation such as the one I have described might have over time. Anointing and crowning are symbols of the conferring of authority, and regal standing and dignity. In an uncanny way my unconscious is attuned to these symbols. The Christian gospel is one of radical equality, every one baptized into Christ is king and priest to God. To appropriate my royalty and priesthood by experiencing in prayer my anointing and crowning with the fire of the Holy Spirit is a profoundly counter-cultural act. I defy the world, which only recognizes my banal identity as consumer and citizen, and I defy my own cowardly low self-esteem, disarming voices of self-depreciation and cynicism with a new awareness of the deep honor and majesty bestowed on me by being given the Spirit of Christ. And consider how my understanding of Christian life changes as I know it as fire within me. Not the keeping of rules, not the maintenance of mediocre decency, but living with fire. "I have come to cast fire on the earth." To pray fire and to know fire within is to be readied for action and change. Fire transforms everything it touches. Meditation with the great symbols of Scripture is no mere aesthetic game.

Another example of a great scriptural symbol which cries out for imaginative appropriation in prayer is baptism. The mystery of dying and rising through submersion in water and emergence into the light is lifeless and opaque for millions of Christians who were baptized in infancy and who have observed only the trivialized modern ceremony in which a few drops of water are sprinkled over babies. In prayer we can allow our baptism to come alive for us with power. Quietly absorbing one of the Scripture passages about baptism we then let our hearts reproduce the experience of baptism imaginatively, the stripping down, descent into the water, hearing the words of affiliation and acceptance by the Holy Trinity, the plunge into the depths, the emergence and clothing with the new robe. The early Christians called baptism illumination, enlightenment. The image of baptism sheds light on the whole of life. In imaginative contemplation of the image we allow this light to shine in our hearts.

The other avenue for the exploration of the prayer of gazing leads to the vast range of moments and scenes in Scripture which invite us to be simply present and look. The invitation is sometimes explicit. At the beginning of John's gospel (1:29) the Baptist "saw Jesus coming toward him, and said 'Behold, the Lamb of God, who takes away the sin of the world!'" In simply looking with John at this figure coming towards us we can experience Jesus in his unknown-ness, the stranger who is yet to show us who he is, whom we will come to know because he is coming for us. Towards the end of the gospel there is that moment when Pilate brings Jesus out to the crowd. "So Jesus came out, wearing the crown of thorns and the purple robe. Pilate said to them, 'Here is the man!'" (19:5) It is by looking at this battered, humiliated and yet regal figure that we will come to know who Jesus is, who God is for us and with us.

At the climax of the crucifixion the writer speaks directly to the reader of the crucial importance of actually seeing the piercing of Jesus' body, and invites us to look and to know what it means. "But one of the soldiers pierced his side with a spear, and at once there came out blood and water. He who saw it has borne witness—his testimony is true, and he knows that he tells the truth—that you also may believe. For these things took place that the scripture might be fulfilled, 'Not a bone of him shall be broken.' And again another scripture says, 'They shall look on him whom they have pierced'" (19:34-37). But there need not be a direct invitation like this. We can be alert to any Scripture passage which presents us with a significant event, scene, movement, or sign which we might contemplate. The range of possibilities is vast, from the spell-binding scene of the Transfiguration to the moment when the beloved disciple went into the tomb where the grave clothes lay empty, "and he saw and believed."

Here are some guidelines for the practice of this kind of prayer.

1   Since this is the stillest and simplest kind of prayer there is much less to occupy the mind, and so we are more vulnerable to distraction. The preparatory relaxation and the postures which enable attentiveness are especially recom-

mended. It can often be helpful to begin by resting the eyes on a simple object evocative of the image we are meditating on, such as a candle, a bowl of water, a stone.

2   Although there is no strict method to this kind of praying, which can unfold in hundreds of ways, there is an underlying movement in which the image or scene is drawn from outside into the heart. First we let the image or scene attract all our senses and imagination. Then we close our eyes and allow the image to be reproduced in the heart.

3   Allow yourself to converse freely with God if that is how you are moved. But if you feel drawn into silent awareness do not disturb yourself.

4   Do not be surprised if there comes a moment in the prayer time when the image or scene fades right away, and you are left only with an obscure awareness of God's presence. In the Transfiguration the disciples entered the cloud. When the image has done its work the Spirit can gently remove it. The images are not God, only means for God to touch us. This experience will become more frequent if God is leading us along the path of contemplative prayer. Then we have to learn to accept without fear as a gift times of being in Christ with God but "in the dark."

5   Allow yourself to return to certain images again and again as long as they seem to draw you. This is far more beneficial than interrupting the process of assimilation by searching for new ones.

10

Practice, Patience And Progress

So much wise teaching about prayer from past and present spiritual guides could be handed on here that it is difficult to keep an introduction to meditation with Scripture within bounds. So much more could be said. However, even the Bible itself comes to its last page. In fact the last word Scripture has to say provides the best note with which to round off these brief guidelines. "The Spirit and the Bride say 'Come.' And let him who hears say, 'Come.' And let him who is thirsty come, let him who desires take the water of life without price." The final paragraph of the Revelation to John rings with the invitation to come, crying out to Christ, "Come, Lord Jesus," and beckoning us to come to satisfy our deepest needs by coming to him. To desire to pray with the Word of God in Scripture is to feel the pull of that invitation, and the urge to keep on calling Christ to come. What we need most of all in answering that invitation was suggested by John at the very beginning of his book, where he identifies himself in this striking way: "I John, your brother, who share with you in Jesus the tribulation and the kingdom and the patient endurance" (1:9).

The great teachers of prayer are unanimous in affirming the fundamental importance of patience in the life of the spirit. We may lack any number of qualities as we begin to pray seriously and regularly but unless we learn to practice patience, an undramatic persistence and resilience, prayer will not take root. With patience we learn to surrender our lust for quick results, to view life in the long term, to be compassionate towards ourselves, and to wait upon God. As soon as we spell out what patient endurance is we realize how completely at odds it is with the values promoted by contemporary western culture. It is this clear awareness that what we seek is thoroughly counter-cultural and non-conformist that enables us to make our own the warnings of Scripture about "being crucified to the world." John tells us that our life in Jesus seeking to live in the hidden sovereignty of God means tribulation, a constant living in contradiction to the goals and values taken for granted in the world, and in vulnerability to its opposition. It is no coincidence that the virtue vital for a life of prayer is equally essential to the revolution in human awareness which alone can halt the plundering of the earth and the ravaging of the environment.

Patience is a gift of God to be asked for. It is so much in God's hands that God is called in Scripture "the God of patience" (Rom. 15:5), and so basic that it is the last word in Jesus' most famous parable, the sower (a better title would be the parable of the various soils): "And as for that in the good soil, they are those who, hearing the word, hold it fast in an honest and good heart, and bring forth fruit *with patience*" (Luke 8:15). As we ponder this saying we realize how directly it speaks to us who are seeking to take in the living word through meditative prayer.

Patience is needed in the first place for the simple enterprise of acquiring the new habit of meditative prayer. At one level meditation is simply a habit of regularly resorting to a private place for periods of focused attention. It is healthy to regard it in a down-to-earth way as a physical rhythm and practice to be learnt like the habit of taking regular exercise. We need patience in getting into the practice because there is often little support for it in our surroundings and because there is a weight of inertia holding our present pattern of life in place, one in which prayer perhaps is left to odd moments. But we also need patience because the attempt to acquire a meditative practice reveals sooner or later how much we do not want to pray. Some people are quite shocked to find out how much reluctance can well up when the time they had intended to meditate comes round. But this inertia and distaste for prayer is not a personal failing for which we must berate ourselves as much as a taste of our common fallenness, our common remoteness from the love of God, and the fear we share of being loved absolutely. We cannot hope to escape all of a sudden from this basic human condition of reluctance and sluggishness. In prayer we must come as we are to God for healing, and that frequently means in our humiliating condition of sluggishness.

More than this we should expect the spiritual forces of negativity which seek to counteract the love and creativity of God to obstruct our attempts to hold the word fast in our hearts; after the sowing "the devil comes and takes away the word" from some hearts. As our fidelity to the practice of meditation is threatened by feelings of "not being in the

Practice, Patience and Progress

mood" and of boredom at the prospect of prayer, it is important to recognize that our all-too-human inertia is being
exploited by "the enemy of human nature" which dreads our
coming home to the love of God. It helps to be as candid
with God as possible about our struggles, being perfectly
open about how we desire to pray and do not desire to pray,
and asking quite simply and regularly for help in being
steadfast.

We need patience, too, in the sense of tolerance for the
inadequacies of our early attempts to meditate. The deadly
enemy of prayer is that spirit of hasty perfectionism which
angrily spurns some project because we cannot master it in
a few attempts.

It is surprising how few people really penetrate to the
heart of the parental images of God, the names "Father," and
(as we are now gaining in freedom to say) "Mother." Is it not
the most universal characteristic of ordinary good parents to
take a special delight in the earliest attempts of their
children to walk, speak, sing, draw? The clumsiness of their
first efforts is found intensely endearing rather than embarrassing. In the prophecy of Hosea, God is compared to a
mother teaching her child to walk with the help of one of
those little harnesses (11:1-9). How many of us have really
accepted the implication that God, far from being a critic of
our prayer as beginners, is as overjoyed by our wavering
efforts as a mother is entranced by the halting steps of her
child, as delighted by our clumsy words as a father hearing
his name uttered by his daughter for the first time? If our
attempts to practice meditative prayer have an initial
awkwardness, and some of them get nowhere or seem very

Chapter Ten

rudimentary, we must lay aside all judgment and perfectionism and rely on the accepting motherly heart of God. It
would be just like God to take more joy in our practicing the
scale of prayer than in the proficient meditations of the
experienced.

Patience is needed in learning to cope with distractions
and wandering thoughts in meditation. We shall always have
distractions in our prayer, lots of "static" in the reception,
but we can learn to make choices which reduce their power
to interfere with our communing with God. The guidelines
in previous chapters distill some traditional wisdom for minimizing distractions, but it will take time and patience to
absorb them. If you are seriously troubled by distractions in
prayer you may be neglecting a particular recommendation.
It is typical, for example, for beginners to try to get down at
once to the scriptural passage and dive into prayer immediately. But the momentum of the mental fly-wheel continues
to spin it, and preoccupations go on whirling around. It
would be much better to slow it right down through five
minutes of relaxation and simple gestures and words of
preparation. In the meditation itself we try to cultivate an
attitude which allows the distractions to float past without
getting worked up about them and without reaching to bring
them on board. It seldom works to try to shout them away
or argue with them. Instead, after noticing them, we "look
over their shoulders" back to the passage, the story, the place,
the image we were praying with, or we take up the word or
phrase our hearts had been centered on. Quite a bit of our
praying consists of dropping fascinating thoughts, fantasies
and memories to return it to where we were with God, which

can often seem duller. If we take the trouble to imagine what prayer seems like to God, we might realize that a prayer time made up of dozens of these self-denying movements of return to the simple word we were seeking to hear might be a far more precious offering of faith and love in God's eyes than a meditation which gratifies our egos by going more serenely.

Having said this, it is important to grasp that what we might try to brush aside as a distraction can often be the Holy Spirit's real agenda for our prayer. If I keep on regurgitating my anger and irritation with a colleague when I am trying to pray, it may be because I am refusing to acknowledge my anger and neglecting to pray about my colleague and our relationship. The Spirit is insisting that I deal with my anger and not escape from it. We must ask ourselves whether we are prepared to make our most insistent and obstrusive distractions the topic of prayer. It is very common indeed for sexual fantasies to well up in prayer. It is almost never appropriate to spin them out in the prayer time, but God may be responsible for the intrusion of the issue of sexuality into our prayer. Even sophisticated and self-aware believers who do not appear in the least prudish never pray about their sexuality, never give thanks for it or articulate their struggles with Christ. Conventional religion has driven a deep rift between the divine and the erotic. In prayer we are vulnerable enough for the Spirit to try to get us to accept our sexuality as sacred, and to recognize that our erotic passion, often only partially satisfied in our human relationships, can be the fuel for a fiery love of God.

Finally, we need patience to remain undisturbed by the experience of simply being unable to pray. Quite often, even

Chapter Ten

when we are reasonably rested and otherwise things are well with us, nothing comes in prayer. Our feelings and words seem dried up at the source, and the Scripture we read evokes no response whatever. God seems silent and absent. It is tempting to resort to self-disparagement and become angry and frustrated at our inability to pray. As always, this is an error. Conversations have silences. We do not have access to God by simply turning on a tap whenever we want. God frequently stays hidden and we cannot often tell why. If it seems obvious in a prayer time that it is going to be one of those days when the fire will not light no matter how many matches we strike, it is usually best to stay put in our prayer posture for the same length of time we had set aside for prayer and put up with our distractions and impotence without losing our sense of humor. In this way we patiently keep our discipline intact. Afterwards we can get up with the same feelings a sentry has when he goes off duty after a shift during which no one sought entry. Nothing happened, but we were there ready in case someone came. As we grow in maturity we begin to realize that these experiences of spiritual poverty are essential if we are to grow in dependence and trust in God. Prayer is not within our power to guarantee or master; it is always a gift.

As for progress in prayer, that is God's gift and each person's path is unique. There is much to be gained from reading classic writings, but personal guidance is a great boon. Various forms of spiritual direction are becoming more available to ordinary seekers at this time. We can be greatly helped by belonging to a group of people who trust each other and share their current spiritual experience so that together they can discern how God seems to be at work. Two friends who are serious about their spiritual exploration can help each other by sharing their experience. At times of transition and special development of your relationship with God it may be ideal to have a spiritual director, a mature woman or man of prayer who is qualified to help you understand the meaning of your experience of prayer and can guide you in learning how to interpret the signs of God's presence in your whole life.

Even if you live in a place where there is no access to qualified spiritual directors, you may benefit greatly from going to a retreat house to make a directed retreat. This is a period of silence and seclusion lasting from three to eight days in which you are free to pray for some hours each day. You will have several interviews during the retreat with a director. In these she or he will suggest approaches to use in your prayer in the day ahead and will give you the opportunity to report how your prayer went so that together you can discern just how God is inviting you and reaching out to you, and how you are responding. Directed retreats can result in a remarkable intensification of our awareness of the Lord, and the concentrated spiritual direction we receive can give a new impetus to our progress in Christ. Your local Catholic diocese should be able to advise you where to get information about retreat houses where directed retreats are offered. Likewise the Episcopal clergy may be able to put you in touch with Anglican and ecumenical retreat houses with the same ministry.

I began this book by asking you, the reader, to pause and consider why you had chosen to read it and what you were

Chapter Ten

seeking. Now you have finished this first section of introductory teaching, I suggest you allow yourself some time to reflect on your reactions to the chapters one by one. Have the opening chapters helped you to believe that the attraction to prayer comes from the Spirit already at work in you? Do you have a sense that meditation is a way of *experiencing* intimacy with the God who dwells within you as Spirit, keeps company with you in your humanness, chooses you in love as the Son, embraces you totally as Father and Creator? Have you been given enough clues about the many ways God can speak through the stories, words and images of Scripture and touch us deeply? Do you feel drawn to experiment with any of the ways of meditation for which guidance has been offered? Do you need to return to a particular section to assimilate it further in order to make it more your own?

If you have taken to heart the counsel given about the best kind of setting for meditative prayer, and made the decisions which will open up time and space for it in your life, then you are ready for this new adventure. I have already suggested ways of choosing passages to pray with and you may want to follow up on these suggestions. Section Two of the book offers you more resources for choosing passages to pray with. By looking through some of them you may open yourself to some clues about how God wants to open a new conversation with you now.

Practice, Patience and Progress

PART II
Themes For Prayer

Introduction

The following thematic clusters of Scripture passages are designed to be invitations to prayer helpful for those who are not yet very familiar with the Scriptures. Passages are captioned to suggest one of the many possible angles from which they could be approached. Where single verses are quoted, they are meant to be taken not as isolated proof-texts but as clues to the tenor of the whole passage. It should be understood that when you actually get down to pray with the passage, some other feature than the verse I have highlighted may well prove to be more important for you.

Hundreds of such clusters of passages could be compiled as the possibilities are endless. No attempt has been made to cover the range of the biblical revelation and the resources of the Old Testament have scarcely been touched. Within some of the themes you may feel drawn to choose one or two of the passages suggested. In others you may want to use most of them in sequence.

The subjects overlap and are not listed in a very strict order, but the first eleven themes spring from human feelings and needs. Then themes dealing with God's action and revelation follow. The last five invite meditation on some

Part II

aspects of discipleship.

If from your own knowledge of the Bible other passages than the ones I have suggested start springing to mind that is a measure of the success of these exercises, rather than their failure, since they are meant to stimulate your own exploration, not replace it.

Those who assist the prayer life of others in retreats and spiritual direction build up a repertoire of passages of proven potency. You may recognise those I have found to be most powerful in giving and receiving spiritual direction by the way they reappear in a number of the clusters.

There are other resources for finding Scripture for meditation, of equal or greater value. The first is, of course, attentive listening to the reading of Scripture during worship. Often the word of God strikes home to us only as it comes to us as a living voice rather than a printed page. If a passage specially arrests your attention make a note of it and jot the reference down so you can use it in your prayer. The availability of the New Testament recorded on tape cassettes creates interesting new possibilities for hearing the Scriptures in order to become increasingly familiar with them.

You may wish to obtain a concordance to the Bible. A concordance lists all the words used in a particular translation of the Scriptures in alphabetical order and tells you where to find all the verses in which it occurs, giving a brief snippet of each. In order to find a passage it is sufficient to recall one significant word from it, then you can look that up as in a dictionary, and scan the quotations listed until you find the reference you are looking for. A handy selective concordance is *The Oxford Concise Concordance to the*

Revised Standard Version (Oxford University Press). A complete concordance is *Eerdmans Analytical Concordance to the Revised Standard Version*. Eerdmans also publishes an updated edition of the *Analytical Concordance to the Holy Bible* by Robert Young, which is based on the King James version.

Standing In The Need Of Prayer

"The Spirit helps us in our weakness."
"We do not know how to pray as we ought, but the Spirit himself intercedes for us with sighs too deep for words." Rom. 8:26, 27

Jesus teaches the disciples to pray.
The Lord's prayer, and the parable of the man who needed bread in the middle of the night. Luke 11:1-13

Don't lose heart and give up.
The parable of the widow who persisted until her case was heard. Luke 18:1-8

No need for many words.
Your Father knows what you need before you ask.
Matt. 6:5-34

Part II

156

God knows you intimately already.
"Lord, you have searched me out and known me; you
know my sitting down and my rising up; you discern my
thoughts from afar."   Ps. 139

No need for intensity or sophistication.
Like a child upon its mother's breast.   Ps. 131

The courage to ask.
"Ask and it will be given you; seek and you will find."
                                                   Luke 11:5-13

"Lord, help me!" —The Syrophoenician woman who
could not be shaken off in her quest for healing for her
daughter.   Mark 7:24-30

"Ask and you will receive, that your joy may be full."
                                          John 14:12-20;16:23-33

"Be Still and Know That I Am God."

*We are conditioned to maintain control, to take charge of
situations, to do the talking. Prayer means surrender and a
readiness to return to a simpler state of openness and attentiveness
to a God whose "still, small voice" we tend to drown with our
restless noisiness.*

Themes for Prayer

"One thing is needful."
Jesus reassures Martha that her sister Mary is not being
selfish or lazy in seizing the opportunity for intimate conversation. Nothing could please him more.   Luke 10:38-42

The burning bush.
Moses has to turn aside from his usual path to investigate
the bush. "When the Lord saw that he turned aside to see,
God called to him out of the bush, 'Moses!'"
Exodus 3:1-14

"Speak, Lord, for thy servant hears."
Samuel is encouraged to tell the Lord that he is ready to
receive his message.   1 Sam. 3:1-11

A still, small voice.
The Lord is not heard in uproar. Elijah must listen for the
gentlest of voices.   1 Kings 19:8-13

Returning and rest, quietness and trust.
"Your ears shall hear a voice behind you, saying, 'This is
the way, walk in it.'"   Isaiah 30:15-21

God's message will reach its goal in our hearts.
"My word that goes forth from my mouth . . . shall not
return to me empty."   Isaiah 55

Let Christ Reveal Himself to You as an Impassioned Human Being

Jesus knows stress and temptation.
Jesus tempted in the wilderness.   Luke 4:1-13

"For we have not a high priest who is unable to sympathize with us in our weaknesses, but one who in every respect has been tempted as we are."   Heb. 4:14-5:10

Jesus knows anger and frustration.
He drives the dealers out of the temple.   Mark 11:15-19

He assails Peter for contradicting his commitment to the path of suffering, "Get behind me, Satan!"

Mark 8:27-33

Jesus is grieved and enraged at the rigidity of the religious authorities.   Mark 3:1-6

"O faithless generation, how long am I to . . . bear with you?"   Mark 9:14-29

Jesus groans with frustration at the misguidedness of the Pharisees and the stupidity of the disciples.

Mark 8:11-21

Jesus had to struggle with limitations.
Crushed and overwhelmed by the demands of the needy, Jesus has to get into a boat. His family thinks he has gone mad and come to get him. He has no leisure even to eat, and he has to escape to be alone, to rest and to pray.

Mark 3:7-35; 6:30-56

Themes for Prayer

Jesus needed the solace of intimacy.
Jesus won't let Martha draw Mary away from his company.
The opportunity for deep, quiet conversation doesn't
come often.   Luke 10:38-42

At the last supper, as he prepares for the ordeal of betrayal
and death, he needs the disciple he loved to lie close to
his breast.   John 13:12-30

Jesus experiences conflict with his family.
"Son, why have you treated us so? Behold, your father and
I have been looking for you anxiously."   Luke 2:41-51

"O woman, what have you to do with me? My hour has
not yet come."   John 2:1-12

Jesus' family and friends come to get him because they
think he has gone mad.   Mark 3:20-35

*Jesus is moved by demonstrations of tenderness and
gratitude.*
He welcomes the extravagance of women who, on two oc-
casions, anoint him with their perfume.
                                   Luke 7:36-50; Mark 14:3-9

Jesus knows anguish and desolation.
He "was deeply moved in spirit and troubled" as he joins
in the grieving of his friends over the death of Lazarus.
                                                John 11:1-44

The agony in the garden of Gethsemane.
                                                Mark 14:32-50

Let Christ Reveal Himself to You As the Risen One

The Resurrection Appearances

To Mary Magdalene. She recognises him when he says to her, "Mary." John 20:1-18

To the women who had come to the tomb. "Do not be afraid; go and tell my brethren to go to Galilee, and there they will see me." Matt. 28:1-10

To a couple returning to Emmaus. Jesus interprets the Scriptures to them and is recognised by the way he blesses and breaks bread with them in their home.

Luke 24:28-35

To the disciples assembled in the upper room. "'Peace be with you.' When he had said this he showed them his hands and his side." Luke 24:36-49; John 20:19-25

To Thomas, whose doubt turns to faith at the sign of the wounds of the Risen Christ: "My Lord and my God!"

John 20:24-29

To Peter and the disciples by the Sea of Tiberias. "'Lord, you know that I love you.' Jesus said to him, 'Tend my sheep.'" John 21

To the disciples in Galilee. "Lo, I am with you always, to the close of the age." Matt. 28:16-20

To Saul on the Damascus Road. "Saul, Saul, why do you persecute me? It hurts you to kick against the goads. . . . I am Jesus." Acts 26:12-23

Lift up your heart! Contemplate the Risen Christ in the glory of the Father.
"Father, I desire that they also, whom thou hast given me, may be with me where I am, to behold my glory."

John 17

"Seek the things that are above, where Christ is, seated at the right hand of God. . . . For you have died, and your life is hid with Christ in God." Col. 3:1-4

As his opponents prepare to kill him Stephen sees, with the eyes of faith, Christ in glory at the right hand of God. Acts 7:54-8:1

The Risen Christ comes to us.
"And when I go and prepare a place for you, I will come again and will take you to myself, that where I am you may be also." John 14

"I will not leave you desolate; I will come to you. Yet a little while, and the world will see me no more, but you will see me; because I live, you will live also."

"I will see you again and your hearts will rejoice, and no one will take your joy from you." John 16

"Behold, I stand at the door and knock; if any one hears my voice and opens the door, I will come in to him."

Rev. 3:20-22

Christ in glory intercedes for us all.
"He is able for all time to save those who draw near to God through him, since he always lives to make intercession for them." Heb. 7:21-8:2

Part II

"Who is to condemn? Is it Christ Jesus, who died, yes, who was raised from the dead, who is at the right hand of God, who indeed intercedes for us?" Rom. 8:28-39

The Heart of the Risen Christ is ablaze with zeal for our faithful response.
John's vision of the Lord in splendor. "I am the first and the last, and the living one; I died, and behold I am alive for evermore." Rev. 1

The Risen Christ judges and encourages the churches.
Rev. 2,3

Christ Dwells in You

"He who eats my flesh and drinks my blood abides in me, and I in him." John 6:25-65

"If a man loves me, he will keep my word, and my Father will love him, and we will come to him and make our home with him." John 14:18-24

"I am the true vine. . . . He who abides in me, and I in him, he it is that bears much fruit." John 15:1-11

"How great among the Gentiles are the riches of the glory of this mystery, which is Christ in you, the hope of glory." Col. 1:24-29

Jesus' great prayer for his friends.
"I made known to them thy name, and I will make it known, that the love with which thou has loved me may be in them, and I in them."   John 17

Christ dwells in us, His Spirit is in us.
"If Christ is in you, although your bodies are dead because of sin, your spirits are alive because of righteousness."
                                                    Rom. 8:9-17

"By this we know that he abides in us, by the Spirit which he has given us."   1 John 3:19-4:21

Christ is my new Self.
"It is no longer I who live, but Christ who lives in me."
                                                    Gal. 2:19-21

We must let Christ into our hearts again and again.
"Behold, I stand at the door and knock; if anyone hears my voice and opens the door, I will come in to him and eat with him, and he with me."   Rev. 3:15-22

The Universal Christ

Let Christ make himself known to you as the Creative Wisdom of God, the Word which spoke the universe into existence, the Life and Light which sustains it, the Source of all truth wherever it is found, the Focus on which all reality converges, the Unity in which all Creation will be reconciled. Worship him in your heart as the Heart which beats in and through everything.

The Word summons the World into being.
"And God said, 'Let there be light'; and there was light."

Gen. 1

God's Wisdom, here personified as feminine, is Creative Love at play in the world.

Prov. 8:22-31; Wisd. 7:22-8:5

"The Word became flesh."
"He was in the world, and the world was made through him." John 1:1-19

"He reflects the glory of God and bears the very stamp of his nature, upholding the universe by his word of power."

Heb. 1:1-4

"All things were created through him and for him. He is before all things, and in him all things hold together."

Col. 1:15-20

All creation will come together in him.
"His purpose which he set forth in Christ . . . to unite all things in him, things in heaven and things on earth." Eph. 1; Col. 1:9-20

The cross reveals that suffering love upholds creation.
"Christ crucified . . . the power of God and the wisdom of God." 1 Cor. 1:18-30

Let Jesus Make Himself Known to You As Servant

Has Jesus ceased to be a servant? Can you allow yourself to be served by Jesus? Do you always have to be looking up to him? What if he wants to be at your feet looking up to you, wanting to minister to your needs, and attend to your cares?

Jesus washes the feet of his disciples. "If I do not wash you, you have no part in me."   John 13:1-11

Jesus prepares breakfast for the weary disciples who have toiled all night.   John 21:1-14

The Son of man came to serve.   Mark 10:35-45

"He will come and serve them." What kind of master is this who, on his return, will wait on his own staff?   Luke 12:35-40

"He emptied himself, taking the form of a servant."
                    Phil. 2:1-11

His servanthood foreshadowed. "Behold my servant . . . my chosen, in whom my soul delights . . . a bruised reed he will not break, and a dimly burning wick he will not quench."
                    Is. 42

"Surely he has borne our griefs . . . upon him was the chastisement which made us whole."   Is. 50,52,53

Jesus Yearns to Draw You to Himself

"Come to me all who labor and art heavy-laden, and I will give you rest."   Matt. 11:25-30

"And I, when I am lifted up from the earth, will draw all men to myself."   John 12:20-36

Jesus, dying on the cross, thirsts for your response to his love.   John 19:28-30

The lost sheep, the lost coin.   Luke 15:3-10

Jesus does not let Zacchaeus keep a safe distance. He wants to meet him and come home with him.

Luke 19:1-10

His love is greater than any lover's. "Arise, my love, my fair one, and come away; for lo, the winter is past."

Song of Sol. 2:10-17

Come to Know The Spirit Who Lives in You

The Holy Spirit is already in you through baptism. Come to know the one you already possess through patient, expectant prayer on the images of the Spirit's mysterious presence, life and action.

Themes for Prayer

The Creator Spirit, Life-giving breath of God.
"In the beginning God created the heavens and the earth
. . . and the Spirit of God was moving over the face of the
waters."   Gen. 1

"God formed man of dust from the ground, and breathed
into his nostrils the breath of life."   Gen. 2:1-9

"O Lord, how manifold are your works! in wisdom you
have made them all. . . . You send forth your Spirit, and
they are created."   Ps. 104

God's Spirit is everywhere, inescapable love!
"Where can I go then from your Spirit? Where can I flee
from your presence?"   Ps. 139

*The Creator Spirit recreates our humanity in the
womb of Mary.*
"The Holy Spirit will come upon you . . . therefore the
child to be born will be called holy, the Son of God."

Luke 1:26-38

*The Spirit anoints Jesus, confirms his Sonship at
his baptism.*
"Immediately he saw the heavens opened and the Spirit
descending upon him like a dove."   Mark 1:1-14

*The Spirit drives Jesus into the testing-place of
solitude and strife.*
"And Jesus, full of the Holy Spirit, returned from the Jordan, and was led by the Spirit for forty days in the wilderness."   Luke 4:1-14

The Spirit-filled Christ is God's prophet of justice and freedom.
"The Spirit of the Lord is upon me, because he has anointed me to preach good news to the poor."   Luke 4:14-30; Is. 61

"And the Spirit of the Lord shall rest upon him, the spirit of wisdom and understanding, the spirit of counsel and might."   Is. 11:1-10

"Behold my servant, whom I uphold, my chosen, in whom my soul delights; I have put my Spirit upon him, and he will bring forth justice to the nations."   Is. 42

The Spirit wells up in Jesus in praise.
"He rejoiced in the Holy Spirit and said, 'I thank thee, Father, Lord of heaven and earth, that thou hast hidden these things from the wise and understanding and revealed them to babes.'"   Luke 10:21-24

The Spirit in Jesus is his power to heal.
"If it is by the Spirit of God that I cast out demons, then the kingdom of God has come upon you."

Matt. 12:15-32

The Resurrection empowers Christ to fill us with the Spirit.
John prophesies that the Coming One "will baptize you with the Holy Spirit."   Mark 1:1-14; John 1:19-34

Jesus tells the Samaritan woman that he is able to give her the living, eternal water, the indwelling Spirit.

John 4:1-30

"For he whom God has sent utters the words of God, for it is not by measure that he gives the Spirit; the Father loves

Themes for Prayer

the Son, and has given all things into his hand."

John 3:31-36

By Christ's absolute self-giving on the Cross the Spirit in
his heart is released into the world. "One of the soldiers
pierced his side with a spear, and at once there came out
blood and water."   John 19; John 7:37-40; 1 John 5:6-12

On the evening of his Resurrection Jesus meets his disciples with peace. "And . . . he breathed on them, and said
to them, 'Receive the Holy Spirit.'"   John 20:19-23

Jesus at the last supper teaches the disciples about the
coming Counsellor, the Spirit of truth. "And I will pray
the Father, and he will give you another Counsellor, to be
with you for ever, even the Spirit of truth . . . you know
him, for he dwells with you, and will be in you."

John 14,15,16

On the day of the Pentecost the gathered disciples are all
filled with the Holy Spirit, the wind and fire of God.

Acts 2

Baptism implants the Spirit in our hearts.
The gift of the Spirit is rebirth into the life of freedom.
"Unless one is born of water and the Spirit, he cannot
enter the Kingdom of God."   John 3

"By one Spirit we were all baptized into one body—Jews
or Greeks, slaves or free—and all were made to drink of
one Spirit."   1 Cor. 12

You who "have believed in him, were sealed with the
promised Holy Spirit, which is the guarantee of our in-

Part II

heritance until we acquire possession of it, to the praise of
his glory." Eph. 1

The Spirit is the giver of Love.
"God's love has been poured into our hearts through the
Holy Spirit which has been given to us." Rom. 5

Love abides, the greatest gift of the Spirit. 1 Cor. 13

**The Spirit includes us in Jesus' intimacy with the
Father.**
"When we cry 'Abba! Father!' it is the Spirit himself bear-
ing witness with our spirit that we are children of God."
Rom. 8; Gal. 4:1-7

The Spirit teaches us in our inmost hearts.
"The Counsellor, the Holy Spirit, whom the Father will
send in my name, he will teach you all things, and bring
to your remembrance all that I have said to you."
John 1:25-30;15:26,27;16:12-15

"Now we have received . . . the Spirit which is from God,
that we might understand the gifts bestowed on us by God
. . . interpreting spiritual truths to those who possess the
Spirit." 1 Cor. 2

**The Spirit enables us to do God's will with freedom
instead of forced conformity.**
"A new heart I will give you, and a new spirit I will put
within you." Ezek. 36:22-36

"A new covenant, not in a written code but in the Spirit. .
. . Where the Spirit of the Lord is, there is freedom."
2 Cor. 3:1-4:6

Themes for Prayer

"If you are led by the Spirit you are not under the law. . . .
The fruit of the Spirit is love, joy, peace, patience, kind-
ness, goodness, faithfulness, gentleness, self-control."

Gal. 5,6

The Living Bread

*In meditating on the Living Bread images of Scripture we allow
ourselves to be the hungry people we are and shake off the pretense
of being satisfied. Our inner hunger tells us there is more to life
than the conventional rewards that pacify the easily satisfied. God
is the nourishment we long for.*

Manna in the desert.
God feeds the wanderers in the desert where human
resourcefulness is no use. But they must depend on God
afresh every day. The manna does not keep. "Give us this
day our daily bread." What do I need today?   Exodus 16

God's wisdom is a feast for the heart.
Listen to Wisdom inviting us to her banquet.

Prov. 9:1-12

Jesus said . . . "My food is to do the will of him who sent
me."   John 4:31-38

The feeding of the Five Thousand.
In the hands of Jesus five loaves and two fish became more
than enough for everyone.   John 6:1-14

The great discourse on the Living Bread.
"I am the bread of life ... unless you eat the flesh of the
Son of man and drink his blood, you have no life in you."
                                                  John 6:21-59

*Jesus give his own self, totally offered to God, as
our food.*
"Take; this is my body. ... This is my blood of the new
covenant, which is poured out for many."   Mark 14:12-25

The eucharist, participation in the Body and Blood of
Christ.   1 Cor. 10:16-22; 11:17-32

*The Risen Christ, incognito, breaks bread at Em-
maus.*
"He was known to them in the breaking of the bread."
                                                  Luke 24:13-35

Jesus, always ready to feed us.
By the lakeside the Risen Christ prepares a meal for the
disciples. "Come and have breakfast."   John 21:1-14

"My Soul Is Athirst for the Living God"

Longing for God in barren places.
"My soul thirsts for you, my flesh faints for you, as in a barren and dry land where there is no water."   Ps. 63

"As the deer longs for the water-brooks, so longs my soul for you, O God."   Ps. 42

God's grace is available in the driest, hardest places.
"Those who go through a desolate valley will find it a place of springs."   Ps. 84

"[God] turned the hard rock into a pool of water and flintstone into a flowing spring."   Ps. 114

God commands Moses to strike the rock to release the spring and quench the thirst of the despairing wanderers.
          Num. 20:2-13

Only God can satisfy this thirst, only Jesus can give what I desire.
"For with you is the well of life . . ."   Ps. 36:5-12

"One of the soldiers pierced his side with a spear, and at once there came out blood and water."   John 19:28-37

Ask God to quench your thirst, strike the rock and come with just your neediness.
"When the poor and needy seek water, and there is none, and their tongue is parched with thirst, I the Lord will answer them."   Is. 41:17-20

"Ho, every one who thirsts, come to the waters; Why do you spend . . . you labour for that which does not satisfy?"

Is. 55

Jesus and the Samaritan woman. "If you knew the gift of God, and who it is that is saying to you, 'Give me a drink,' you would have asked him, and he would have given you living water."

John 4:1-30

"He who believes in me, as the scripture has said, 'Out of his heart shall flow rivers of living water.'"

John 7:37-39

"The river of the water of life, bright as crystal, flowing from the throne of God and of the Lamb. . . . Let him who is thirsty come, let him who desires take the water of life without price."

Rev. 21:5-7; 22

The Light of the Glory of God

"God is light and in him is no darkness at all." Light is supreme amongst the images of God's being and self-giving. The simplest act of watching the dawn, standing in the light of the sun, gazing at a candle flame can admit us into a sense of God's inexhaustible glory. In meditation we return again and again to the mystery of God's limitless creativity, as the one who calls the universe of energy into being: "Let there be light!" We sense in prayer how our own lives are bathed in God's light and reflect it back. Our human vocation is to shine, to be radiant people. As we pray we experience light falling on dark and shadowy places searching us

in judgment and guiding us. Meditating on the images of light we are led to Christ who is the Light of the world.

God, creator of light and life.
"'Let there be light,' and there was light."   Gen. 1:1-2:3

The magnificence of the sun, moon and stars, their light drawing us to God in praise and wonder.

Pss. 19,104; Sir. 43:1-12

The Uncreated Light, the Glory of God.
Every human being who comes into the world is enlightened by it.   John 1

Moses granted a visionary experience of it.

Exod. 33:12-23

Faith seeks its blessing in our lives.
"Lift up the light of your countenance upon us."   Ps. 4

"The Lord is my light and my salvation."   Ps. 27

"In your light we see light."   Ps. 36

Christ is the Light of the World.

John 1; John 8:12

He attracts those who live by truth.   John 3:16-21

The healing of the man born blind reveals the whole meaning of Christ's mission of enlightenment and the drama of judgment.   John 9

"I have come as light into the world, that whoever believes in me may not remain in darkness."

John 12:34-50

Part II

There is no other source of life and glory.
"The city has no need of sun or moon to shine upon it, for the glory of God is its light, and its lamp is the Lamb."
Rev. 21:22-22:5

God's love transforms us, we became radiant ourselves.
After his descent from the mountain Moses' face shines with the divine radiance.   Exod. 34:29-35

The Transfiguration of Jesus on the mountain.
Luke 9:28-36

"We all, with unveiled face, beholding the glory of the Lord, are being changed into his likeness from one degree of glory to another."   2 Cor. 3:7-4:18

"It is the God who said, 'Let light shine out of darkness,' who has shone in our hearts to give the light of the knowledge of the glory of God in the face of Christ."

"Once you were darkness, but now you are light in the Lord; walk as children of light."   Eph. 5:1-20

"God is light and in him is no darkness at all . . . if we walk in the light, as he is in the light, we have fellowship with one another."   1 John 1:5-10

Being A Creature

In prayer we explore again and again what it means to be a creature, to be part of the creation that depends on God moment by moment for its existence and meaning, its movement towards fulfillment. I am the creation in miniature. It is easy to lose the awe of total dependence, to drift away from the awareness of belonging to the magnificent web of life, to lose faith in the continuous, life-giving, sustaining, shaping, urging action of the God who holds all things in life.

Awe at the splendor of creation.
Its mysteries are beyond our grasp.   Job. 38,39

The works of God mesh in an amazing order.

"They do not crowd one another aside, and they will
never disobey his word."   Sir. 16:26-30; 43

God loves and delights in the universe of creation.
"And God saw everything that he had made, and behold,
it was very good."   Gen. 1

"Thou lovest all things that exist, and hast loathing for
none of the things which thou hast made." Wisd. 11:21-26

God delights in the sublime wisdom which crafts the
universe.   Prov. 8:22-31

Human life seems so fragile and precarious, yet uniquely favored by God.
"When I consider your heavens, the work of your fingers. .
. . What is man that you should be mindful of him?"

                    Ps. 8

"There is for all mankind one entrance into life, and a common departure." Wisd. 7:1-6

God "gave to them a few days, a limited time, but granted them authority over things upon the earth." Sir. 17:1-15

Our Maker's all-surpassing Majesty.
"Worthy art thou, our Lord and God, to receive glory and honour and power, for thou didst create all things, and by thy will they existed and were created." Rev. 4

"'He is the all.' Where shall we find strength to praise him? For he is greater than all his works." Sir. 43

"The Lord is the everlasting God, the Creator of the ends of the earth. He does not grow faint or weary, his understanding is unsearchable." Is. 40:12-31

"Bless the Lord, O my soul; O Lord my God, how excellent is your greatness! You are clothed with majesty and splendor. You wrap yourself with light as with a cloak and spread out the heavens like a curtain." Ps. 104

"Praise him, sun and moon; praise him, all you shining stars." Ps. 148

"Bless the Lord, all works of the Lord, sing praise to him and highly exalt him for ever."

Song of the Three Young Men

God is still the shaper of our lives.
He is like a potter moulding clay.
Gen. 2; Is. 45:9-12; Jer. 18:1-10; Rom. 9:20-24

"For we are his workmanship, created in Christ Jesus for good works, which God prepared beforehand, that we should walk in them." Eph. 2:1-10

Christ is the Living Word through whom everything has its being.

"All things were made through him." John 1

"The heir of all things, through whom also he created the world." Heb. 1

All things were created through him and for him.
Col. 1:1-20

"A plan for the fulness of time, to unite all things in him, things in heaven and things on earth." Eph. 1

The suffering world will come to fulfillment.
"The creation itself will be set free from its bondage to decay and obtain the glorious liberty of the children of God." Rom 8:18-25

"Then I saw a new heaven and a new earth. . . . And he who sat upon the throne said, 'Behold, I make all things new.'" Rev. 21

Let the Children Come to Me

In meditation I allow my own self-as-child to be re-embraced by God. I recognize voices within myself that devalue children's experience of God, and forces that push back the hurt child within, refusing to recognise its right to be healed, cherished and blessed. Christ's invitation encourages me to resist them, and to come to him.

Part II

"Who is the greatest?"
"Unless you turn and become like children, you will never enter the kingdom of heaven." Matt. 18:1-5

"Let the children come to me."
"To such belongs the kingdom. . . . And he took them in his arms." Mark 10:13-16

"Little girl, arise."
Jesus brings a little girl back to life who had been given up for dead. Mark 5:22-24; 35-43

There is a kind of damage only prayer can restore.
A terribly sick and vulnerable child is surrounded by powerless, argumentative adults. He is lifted back into life through the touch and prayer of Jesus. Mark 9:14-29

God chooses to speak to a little boy.
It is a little boy, Samuel, to whom God speaks when others are not hearing the word of the Lord. 1 Samuel 3

The faith of a boy not understood.
As a child, Jesus is riveted by the worship and life of the Temple. Even Mary and Joseph are incapable of appreciating the religious experience of their son and react with hurt and bewilderment. Luke 2:41-52

"Like a child upon its mother's breast."
Can we allow ourselves to experience the cradling, nurturing love of God our mother? Psalm 131

Heal Me and I Shall Be Healed!

Through the stories of healing we can allow our inner unhealed selves to be touched by God. Where are the places in your heart which harbor pain and injury? Where is there deadness, where have you been crippled, what are the inner persons from which you recoil?

Do you want to be healed?
Jesus searches into the heart of the paralytic who has grown accustomed to his endless waiting by the pool of Bethzatha.   John 5:1-24

What do you want me to do for you?
Jesus insists that Bartimaeus, the blind beggar, should let his real desire surface and find voice. Faith is aroused in the expression of desire.   Mark 10:46-52

Who touched me?
Jesus wants the healing experience to be a real meeting with him face to face. He insists that the woman just cured of her hemorrhage make herself known so he can welcome and bless her.   Mark 5:25-34

Jesus is not threatened by craziness.
Jesus is not intimidated when he meets the deranged. He meets the challenge of deep-seated sickness with compassion and confidence, and heals a man with an unclean spirit at Capernaum.   Mark 1:21-28

Part II

Even the hopelessly self-destructive and isolated can become whole again.
Jesus restores the lunatic who called himself "Legion."

Mark 5:1-20

Unable to understand people, unable to make them understand me.
A man condemned to silence and isolation is restored to the rich world of communication through Jesus' touch.

Mark 7:31-37

From blankness to the wonder of clear sight.
A man for whom everything was blank is brought by Jesus into the real world of endless diversity.

Mark 8:22-26

A victim from childhood.
Through prayer Jesus heals a boy who has known nothing but pain and isolation from childhood.

Mark 9:14-29

The double-bind of rigidity and guilt.
A man who couldn't move, begins to walk, but only after Jesus has liberated him from guilt.

Mark 2:1-12

Healing: there is no time like the present!
Jesus helps a man with a withered hand. He ignores the authorities who want him to postpone the healing.

Mark 3:1-6

A woman bent in upon herself.
Jesus restores a cramped and distorted life and enables a suffering woman to move freely and relate to people face to face.

Luke 13:10-17

Health and gratitude.
Jesus cures ten lepers, but only one is truly healed—a foreigner who turns back to show his gratitude to Jesus.

Luke 17:11-19

Healing doesn't need to be dramatic or complicated.
Naaman the leper is skeptical at first because Elisha promises a cure through very simple means. He has to learn to trust. 2 Kings 5:1-14

Jesus does not disdain to attend to everyday troubles.
Jesus attends to Peter's mother-in-law's fever.

Mark 1:29-31

Those who deny their need for healing are the really sick.
The Pharisees thought they could see perfectly. Their resentful, faithless reaction to Jesus healing a blind man reveals the darkness they were living in. John 9

The anguish of sickness.
"Hide not your face from me in the day of my trouble."

Pss. 30, 6, 13, 88

The joy of healing and recovery.
"You have rescued my life from death, my eyes from tears, and my feet from stumbling."

Pss. 30, 103, 116

Praying in Pain

Psalms of Affliction.
"My spirit shakes with terror; how long, O Lord, how long?"   Ps. 6

"How long shall I have perplexity in my mind, and grief in my heart, day after day?"   Ps. 13

"My God, my God, why hast thou forsaken me?"   Ps. 22

"Have mercy on me, O Lord, for I am in trouble."   Ps. 31

"Truly, I am on the verge of falling, and my pain is always with me."   Ps. 38

"In the shadow of your wings will I take refuge until this time of trouble has gone by."   Ps. 57

"I am sinking in deep mire, and there is no firm ground for my feet."   Ps. 69

"Do not cast me off in my old age; forsake me not when my strength fails."   Ps. 71

"Has God forgotten to be gracious? Has he, in his anger, withheld his compassion?"   Ps. 77

"I have become like one who has no strength."   Ps. 88

"I lie awake and groan; I am like a sparrow, lonely on a house-top."   Ps. 102

"Out of the depths have I called to you, O Lord; Lord, hear my voice."   Ps. 130

"I look to my right hand and find no one who knows me; I have no place to flee to, and no one cares for me." Ps. 142

Abandoned by God?
"Why is light given to him that is in misery, and life to the bitter in soul?"   Job 3:20-26, Job 23

A man of sorrows and acquainted with grief.
Christ keeps company with those he has made his own in the worst that can befall them.   Is. 53

Christ identifies himself with the suffering.
In the judgment tableau of the sheep and the goats, Christ reveals that he suffers in and with the needy.

Matt. 25:31-46

"My God, my God, why hast thou forsaken me?"
Jesus has been before me into the depths of feeling abandoned. He knows what desolation is.

Mark 15:21-39

I complete what is lacking in Christ's afflictions.
Suffering can be offered as a share in the total ordeal of Christ, a way of transforming evil into good through love.   Col. 1:24-27

God comforts us in affliction, so that we may comfort others.

2 Cor. 1:1-12

Afflicted, but not crushed.
Affliction can become a way of dying with Christ so that we can experience his resurrection life.   2 Cor. 4:7-18

My power is made perfect in weakness.
Paul displays the proofs of his apostolic calling—so many failures, so many setbacks, so much weakness! The power

Part II

of Christ is revealed in the midst of human impotence and struggle. 2 Cor. 11:16-12:10

The sufferings of this present time are not worth comparing with the glory that is to be revealed to us.

Rom 8:18-28

Shall tribulation and distress separate us from the love of Christ?
"No, in all these things we are more than conquerors through him who loved us." Rom 8:28-39

Anguish in the Face of Evil and Suffering

Entering the grief of Jesus.
"O Jerusalem, Jerusalem, killing the prophets. . . . How often would I have gathered your children together as a hen gathers her brood under her wings?" Luke 13:31-35

"And when Jesus drew near and saw the city he wept over it." Luke 19:41-45

The Spirit makes us feel acutely the struggles of the world.
"We know that the whole creation has been groaning in travail together until now . . . we ourselves groan inwardly."

Rom 8:18-25

Sharing the honesty of the prophets and psalmists in their outrage and grief.

"Surely, you behold trouble and misery; you see it and take it into you hand." Ps. 10

"I had almost tripped and fallen, because I envied the proud and saw the prosperity of the wicked." Ps. 73

"Look upon your covenant; the dark places of the earth are haunts of violence." Ps. 74

"How long shall the wicked, O Lord, how long shall the wicked triumph?" Ps. 94

"I writhe in pain! . . . I cannot keep silent; for I hear the sound of the trumpet, the alarm of war."

Jer. 4:18-31; 12:1-4

"Justice is far from us . . . we look for light, and behold, darkness." Is. 59

"Wilt thou restrain thyself at these things, O Lord? Wilt thou keep silent?" Is. 64

God Chose You First

God called us by name and chose us first. Again and again we must abandon the illusion that we must first prove ourselves and earn God's love.

"I have called you by name, you are mine." Is. 43:1-7

"Behold, I have graven you on the palms of my
hands." Is. 49:13-17

"Before I formed you in the womb I knew you, and before
you were born I consecrated you." Jer. 1:1-8

"He who had set me apart before I was born, and had
called me through his grace, was pleased to reveal his Son
to me." Gal. 1:11-17

God "has blessed us in Christ with every spiritual blessing
. . . even as he chose us in him before the foundation of
the world." Eph. 1

"Rejoice that your names are written in heaven."
Luke 10:17-22

"You did not choose me, but I chose you and appointed
you that you should go and bear fruit." John 15:12-17

God gave us to Christ. "Father . . . thine they were, and
thou gavest them to me." John 17

"Those whom he foreknew he also predestined to be con-
formed to the image of his Son . . . and those . . . he also
called; and those whom he called he also justified."
Rom. 8:28-39

Nathanael is taken aback to discover that Jesus already
knows all about him and has chosen him. John 1:43-51

Your Sins are Forgiven,
Enter into the Joy of Your Master

"My son, your sins are forgiven."
A paralysed man is lowered through an opening in the
roof of the crowded house where Jesus is staying. He heals
him and forgives his sins.   Mark 2:1-12

Why does he eat with . . . sinners?
The gift of reconciliation strikes home as Jesus celebrates
in the homes of outcasts and sinners.   Mark 2:13-17

Jesus recruits sinners to be his trusted companions.
"'Depart from me, for I am a sinful man, O Lord'. . . . And
Jesus said to Simon, 'Do not be afraid.'"   Luke 5:1-11

A woman takes the offer of forgiveness to heart and
gatecrashes a party to show her gratitude to Jesus in a
lavish gesture of love.   Luke 7:36-50

The prodigal son.
"While he was yet at a distance, his father saw him and
had compassion, and ran and embraced him."
                                               Luke 15:11-32

The woman taken in adultery.
"Neither do I condemn you; go and sin no more."
                                               John 8:1-12

Jesus invites himself to Zacchaeus' home.
"The Son of man came to seek and to save the lost."
                                               Luke 19:1-10

Part II

190

"Simon, son of John, do you love me?"
After the resurrection Jesus gives Peter the chance to
undo his threefold denial. John 21:15-19

"While we were yet sinners Christ died for us."
Rom. 5; 1 John 4:7-21

"If any one does sin, we have an advocate with the Father,
Jesus Christ the righteous: and he is the expiation for our
sins." 1 John 1:5-2:6

"Happy are they whose transgressions are forgiven, and
whose sin is put away!" Ps. 32

"As far as the east is from the west, so far has he removed
our sins from us." Ps. 103

Let forgiveness flow to those who have wronged you.
"Give, and it will be given to you; good measure, pressed
down, shaken together, running over." Luke 6:27-49

The parable of the unmerciful servant. Matt. 18:21-35

Letting Go of Fear and Anxiety

"Do you not care if we perish?"
The disciples panic during a storm. Jesus challenges them
about their lack of trust. Mark 4:35-41

"Do not be anxious about your life."
The Father knows what you need. Matt. 6:25-31

Walking on water.
Jesus, after inviting Peter to come to him across the water, has to save him from sinking when doubt makes him falter.

Matt. 14:22-33

The energy trapped in anxiety should flow into prayer.
"Have no anxiety about anything, but in everything by prayer and supplication with thanksgiving, let your requests be made known to God."   Phil. 4:4-9

"I lift up my eyes to the hills; from where is my help to come? . . . The Lord shall watch over your going out and your coming in from this time forth for evermore." Ps. 121

"The Lord is my shepherd; I shall not be in want. . . . I shall fear no evil; for you are with me."

Ps. 23

"The Lord is the strength of my life; of whom then shall I be afraid?"   Ps. 27

"In the shadow of your wings I will take refuge until this time of trouble has gone by."   Ps. 57

"Who shall separate us from the love of Christ? Shall tribulation or distress . . . ?   Rom. 8:31-39

"Cast all your anxieties on him, for he cares about you."   1 Pet. 5:6-11

Don't Cling to the Past!

In meditation we are made to face again and again our inertia and fear of where God may be leading us. Often we cling to the past or present because even if there is deadness in it we feel safer holding on to the familiar than stepping out into an open future in which God can do something new in our lives.

Abraham uproots himself in response to God's call.
"By faith . . . he went out, not knowing where he was to go."

Gen. 12:1-9; Heb. 11:8-19

God goes before his people.
"The Lord went before them by day in a pillar of cloud to lead them along the way, and by night in a pillar of fire."

Exod. 13

Jesus challenges some who want to postpone following him.
"No one who puts his hand to the plough and looks back is fit for the kingdom of God." Luke 9:57-62

Possessions can hold us back.
The rich young ruler. Mark 10:17-22

In critical times you must be ready to move on without hesitation.
"Remember Lot's wife." Luke 17:22-37

God knows what your future needs are. Stop worrying.
"Do not be anxious about tomorrow, for tomorrow will be anxious for itself." Matt. 6:25-34

Themes for Prayer

The Risen Christ goes ahead of us.
"Tell his disciples and Peter that he is going before you to
Galilee; there you will see him."   Mark 16

**Instead of living in the past, Christians reach out
for God's future.**
"Forgetting what lies behind and straining forward to
what lies ahead, I press on towards the goal for the prize of
the upward call of God in Christ Jesus."   Phil. 3

The faith of God's pilgrim servants.
"Faith is the assurance of things hoped for, the conviction
of things not seen . . . they were strangers and exiles on
the earth."   Heb. 11

In the race we must look ahead to the goal.
"Looking to Jesus the pioneer and perfecter of our faith,
who for the joy that was set before him endured the cross,
despising the shame."   Heb. 12

Realize Your Gifts, Use Them!

*These passages of Scripture can help us bring to the surface the
way we discount ourselves and scorn ourselves as worthless, or
our fear of the particular creativity and opportunity which God
has given us, or our reluctance to see that our lives only make
sense when our gifts contribute to the building up of God's*

community. We need to hear again that we have a unique role to play in the active network of God's grace.

"Before I formed you in the womb, I knew you."

God's word to Jeremiah tells me that God had a vision for my life from the very beginning. Jer. 1:4-5

The parable of the talents.

The man who was afraid to use what had been given him.
Matt. 25:14-30

Branches are for bearing fruit.

"I chose you . . . that you should go and bear fruit and that your fruit should abide." John 15:1-17

God knows the power and meaning of gifts which seem insignificant to human eyes.

"There is a lad here who has five barley loaves and two fish; but what are they among so many?" John 6:1-14

Jesus sees the drastic generosity behind the widow's contribution of two copper coins. Mark 12:41-44

Every organ in a body has an essential part to play.

"To each is given the manifestation of the Spirit for the common good." 1 Cor. 12

"Grace was given to each of us according to the measure of Christ's gift."

Each one of us has a role in the work of building a new humanity. Eph 4:1-16

"As each has received a gift, employ it for one another, as good stewards of God's varied grace." 1 Pet. 4:8-11

Jealousy is absurd, for all are equal.

"He who plants and he who waters are equal." 1 Cor. 3

"There is neither male nor female; for you are all one in
Christ Jesus."   Gal. 3:23-29
Jesus refuses to allow Peter to question the beloved
disciple's unique vocation.   John 21:20-24

I Am Powerless to Be My Own Saviour

*Our only hope is to abandon the attempt to fix our lives through
schemes and efforts of our own, and let God be God. God has
already done what is necessary to make me whole through the
death and resurrection of Jesus and the giving of the Spirit. All I
need to do is to experience what God has done and is doing for
me.*

I cannot myself produce the good I want in my life.
Paul writes about our impotence to produce the wholeness
and fullness of life for which we yearn.   Rom. 7:15-8:1

**Reliance on status, or religious credentials is a
denial of my radical dependence on God.**
Paul writes about how he had to throw overboard all the
security his religious practice had given him in order to
receive the gift of the "righteousness from God that
depends on faith."   Phil. 3

Part II

196

I can try to make the practice of Christianity a way of "staying in God's good books."
Paul remonstrates with the Galatians for making converts adopt the law of Moses, thus undermining the good news that our standing with God is a gift to be accepted with trust.   Gal. 1-4

"While we were yet helpless, at the right time Christ died for the ungodly."   Rom. 5

It is the poor whom Jesus congratulates!   Matt. 5

Only a word from Jesus is needed for the criminal being executed with him to secure a place in paradise.

Luke 23:39-43

The Fear of Commitment

In meditation our fear of commitment can emerge from the shadow into the light of Christ. In his presence our fear is challenged and our faith aroused.

I need to deal with other things first.
Jesus summons two men to follow him, but they both procrastinate.   Luke 9:59-62

I have responsibilities which take priority.
Jesus loves a wealthy young leader full of good intentions,
but is disappointed when he holds back from giving his
money away and joining the disciples.   Mark 10:17-31

"Where your treasure is, there will your heart be
also."   Luke 12

Jesus tells the story of the guests who all found excuses for
not attending the wedding banquet when it was ready.
                                                        Luke 14:15-35

I'm uncomfortable with extremes.
Many disciples cease to follow Jesus after his hard sayings.
                                                        John 6:52-71

The prophet hears the Lord rebuke disciples who cling to
lukewarm mediocrity: "Would that you were cold or hot!"
                                                        Rev. 3:15-22

"I came to cast fire upon the earth!"   Luke 12:49-56

I prefer to keep a low profile.
"You are the light of the world. A city set on a hill cannot
be hid."   Matt. 5:13-16

Refusing to acknowledge Jesus openly will alienate you
from him in the end.   Luke 12:1-12

I hate being forced to choose.
"No one can serve two masters. . . . The gate is narrow
and the way is hard that leads to life."   Matt. 6:24-7:28

I need proof.
The Pharisees demand a sign. Jesus is agonized by their
lack of faith.   Mark 8

Part II

198

I can't face the consequences of commitment.
"Which of you, desiring to build a tower, does not first sit down and count the cost, whether he has enough to complete it?"   Luke 14:25-34

Conflict

God is my loving antagonist who struggles with me in order to save me from falling away.
Jacob wrestles with a stranger all night and is blessed; it was the angel of the Lord.   Gen. 32:22-32

Saul's vision on the Damascus Road. "It hurts you to kick against the goads," Christ tells him. By opposing Christ he is hurting himself; it is time to surrender.

Acts 26:12-18

The presence of God's power and grace provokes conflict and opposition.
"Do not think that I have come to bring peace on earth; I have come not to bring peace, but a sword. . . . A man's foes will be those of his own household."

Matt. 10:34-39

"If you were of the world, the world would love its own . . . . but I chose you out of the world, therefore the world hates you."   John 15:18-27

"Blessed are you when men hate you, and when they exclude you . . . on account of the Son of man! . . . Woe to you, when all men speak well of you, for so their fathers did to the false prophets."

Luke 6: 20-31; 1 Pet. 4:12-19

Adhering to God puts us in conflict with all the structures and forces of evil in the universe.
"We are not contending against flesh and blood, but against the principalities, against the powers, against the world rulers of this present darkness."   Eph. 6:10-20

Evil will try to sabotage my life with God by putting my personal weak spots to the test.
Jesus is put to the test by Satan after his baptism.

Matt. 4:1-11

Jesus teaches his followers to pray to God to protect them from overwhelming temptation and evil.

Matt. 6:7-13

Jesus tells Peter that Satan had demanded to sift him like wheat.   Luke 22:31-34

Satan is a master of disguise, and temptations can appear to be religious impulses.   2 Cor. 11:1-15

The Mother of my Lord

We are invited to enter into Mary's experience and allow it to shed its wonderful light onto our vocation to bear Christ in our hearts and lives. The pain and the glory of her path tells us of our own. She mysteriously communicates to us in prayer both the strength and beauty of God who gave us birth and the dignity of human life when it is filled with the Holy Spirit.

The Annunciation.
"Behold, I am the handmaid of the Lord; let it be to me according to your word."
Luke 1:26-39

The Visitation.
"Blessed are you among women and blessed is the fruit of your womb!"
Luke 1:39-56

Mary sings of God's amazing choice of her, a sign of God's vindication of the poor and the powerless.

Luke 1:46-55

The journey to Bethlehem, the birth of Jesus and the homage of the shepherds.
"Mary kept all these things, pondering them in her heart."
Luke 2:1-20

The Wise Men visit Mary and Joseph.

Matt. 2:1-12

The Presentation in the Temple.
Simeon and Anna discern the identity of Mary's child and prophesy her own path of suffering.
Luke 2:22-38

The years of childhood.

Luke 2:39-40

Themes for Prayer

Jesus stays behind in the Temple.
Mary is hurt and bewildered by the intensity of Jesus' attraction to the House of God.   Luke 2:41-52

The wedding at Cana.
Mary's care is the catalyst for a miracle before Jesus separates himself from her for his mission. "My mother and my brothers are those who hear the word of God and do it." Mary hears that this kinship and intimacy with Jesus is open to everyone who acts on his message.

Luke 8:19-21

Mary at the Cross.
She enters into her son's agony. At the height of his pain Jesus gives her and the disciple he loved to one another.

John 19:25-42

Mary receives the Spirit of her Ascended Son.
With all the company of believers she enters the new life of Pentecost.   Acts 1:12-14; 2:1-4

Jesus with Women

Jesus yields to the prompting of Mary when the wine runs out at the wedding in Cana.   John 2:1-11

Jesus heals the mother of Peter's wife.   Mark 1:29-31

Part II

Jesus defies convention and befriends the Samaritan woman at the well. His questions probe her innermost longings. Her life is changed. John 4

A woman is healed of a hemorrhage as she secretly touches the hem of his cloak. He insists she come out of her anonymity so he can meet her and congratulate her on her faith. Mark 5:25-34

Jesus heals a little girl who has been given up for dead. Mark 5:21-43

Jesus' intimate companions and supporters are women. Travelling and preaching together in a band, they defy convention in the new-found freedom of the kingdom of God. Luke 8:1-3

Jesus' hideout is penetrated by a Gentile woman who wants her daughter well again. The urgency of her will and the sharpness of her wit captivate Jesus and he performs the healing. Mark 7:24-30

Women bring their girls and boys to be blessed by Jesus. The disciples try to stop them and are rebuked by Jesus, who wants the children with him. Mark 10:13-16

Jesus saves a woman from being stoned to death for adultery. John 8:1-11

Meeting a funeral procession, Jesus has compassion on the widow who has lost her son. He revives him and restores him to his mother. Luke 7:11-17

Jesus shocks his host by tenderly accepting a woman's lavish demonstration of gratitude when she breaks into a dinner party to wash his feet with her tears and anoint

them with perfume. He confirms her faith and the forgiveness she has found.   Luke 7:36-50

Jesus at home with his friends Mary and Martha.

Luke 10:38-42

Jesus deflects a compliment from a woman admirer.

Luke 11:27-28

Jesus heals a woman bent in upon herself. Now upright
she can look people in the face again.   Luke 13:10-17

Jesus is full of admiration for the incomparable trust of a
poverty-stricken widow. In contributing the minimum
donation she is giving away all she has to live on.

Luke 21:1-4

Jesus wrestles with grief and death when his beloved Mary
and Martha lose their brother Lazarus. He brings Lazarus
back to life.   John 11

The threat of death now hanging over Jesus, Mary anoints
him with the ointment she had been saving.

John 12:1-8

The women of Jerusalem grieve and protest as Jesus is
forced to drag his cross to the place called "The Skull."

Luke 23:26-31

Only his mother, his friend and the women who had been
his companions have the courage to stay with him as he
dies in slow agony.   John 19

The women are the first to meet Jesus arisen from the
dead. Jesus makes himself known to Mary of Magdala.

John 20:1-18

Peter: The Making of a Disciple

Through some weeks of prayer we can keep company with Peter as he learns who Jesus is, and what it means to love him above all else, to suffer for him, and to draw others to him. We can experience Jesus' love for him with all his impetuosity and weaknesses. In the journey we can learn how well Jesus knows us and how he perseveres with us until we can say with all our heart "Yes, Lord, you know that I love you."

The call of Peter.
Simon's brother Andrew comes to Jesus after John the Baptist has declared him to be the Lamb of God. Andrew brings Simon to Jesus, who gives him the new name Peter, "Rock." John 1:35-42

"Depart from me, for I am a sinful man, O Lord. . . . Do not be afraid; henceforth you will be catching men." Luke 5:1-11

Discovering who Jesus is.
Jesus walks over the lake. Peter goes to him. Jesus saves him when he is overwhelmed by doubt. Matt. 14:22-33

Peter identifies Jesus as God's Son, but refuses to believe in the way of suffering and death Jesus announces as his destiny. Jesus confirms his recognition but attacks him fiercely for his denial of the way of the cross. Matt. 16:13-28

The transfiguration of Jesus. Luke 9:28-36

Learning the new life.
A fantastic proposal by Jesus has a message about trusting that God will provide. Matt. 17:24-27

Themes for Prayer

Readiness to forgive should be limitless.   Matt. 18:21-22

What reward will there be for following Jesus?
Mark 10:23-31

The lessons of the cleansing of the temple and the cursing
of the fig tree.   Mark 11

Training for endurance in the face of crisis and conflict.
Mark 13

Desertion and Denial.

At first Peter tries to prevent Jesus from washing his feet. .
. . Jesus predicts his denial.   John 13

Peter falls asleep in Gethsemane. At the arrest he strikes
out and then flees. Peter denies Jesus three times when
challenged in the courtyard of the high priest.

Mark 14

The Risen Lord and the new beginning.

The empty tomb and the appearance of Jesus in the upper
room.   John 20

Another immense catch of fish at the bidding of the
stranger who turns out to be Jesus. Jesus allows Peter to
undo his denial with a threefold declaration of love. Peter
is told to expect to surrender his life in martyrdom.

John 21

Witness and Apostle.

The coming of the Spirit and the proclaiming of the good
news.   Acts 1,2

The inclusion of the Gentiles.   Acts 10,11,15

Imprisonment and escape.   Acts 12:1-17

Part II

Peter's radicalism falters and Paul has to challenge him to
resume his commitment.   Gal. 2

The mature teaching of the Church's Rock.   1 Peter

Ministry and Discipleship

The God who calls.
"Consider your call . . . not many of you were wise accord-
ing to worldly standards, not many were powerful. . . .
God chose what is low and despised in the world."

                                               1 Cor. 1,2

"I thank thee, Father . . . that thou hast hidden these
things from the wise and understanding and revealed
them to babes."   Luke 10

The call of Moses at the burning bush: "I am slow of
speech and of tongue."   Exod. 3,4

The call of Isaiah: "Woe is me! . . . I am a man of unclean
lips."   Is. 6

The call of Jeremiah: "Do not say, 'I am only a youth'; for
to all to whom I send you you shall go."   Jer. 1

The call of Peter: "Depart from me, for I am a sinful man,
O Lord."   Luke 5:1-11

The call of Andrew, Philip and Nathanael: "How do you
know me?"   John 1

The call of Levi.   Luke 5:27-32

Themes for Prayer

After praying all night, Jesus chooses the twelve.   Luke 6

"You did not choose me, but I chose you and appointed you that you should go and bear fruit."   John 15

The call of Saul, the persecutor.   Acts 26:12-23; Gal. 1

Agents of God's compassion.
Sharing Christ's ministry of emancipation and healing.
                                                    Luke 4:14-44

"He had compassion for them, because they were . . . like sheep without a shepherd."   Matt. 9:35-38

Instructions for ministry.   Matt. 10, Luke 10

"Whoever would be first among you must be slave of all."
                                                    Mark 10:35-45

The example of the footwashing.   John 13

"Feed my sheep."   John 21

"Servants of Christ and stewards of the mysteries of God."
                                                    1 Cor. 4

"Ambassadors for Christ, God making his appeal through us."   2 Cor. 5

"We were gentle among you, like a nurse taking care of her children . . . affectionately desirous of you."   1 Thess. 2

Varieties of service, but the same Lord.
"Having gifts that differ according to the grace given to us."   Rom 12, 1 Cor. 12,13

Building up the body of Christ.   Eph. 4

Some are "planters," some "waterers." Both are equal; God is responsible for the growth.   1 Cor. 3

Part II

God's grace in our fragility and humanness.

"I decided to know nothing among you except Jesus
Christ and him crucified. And I was with you in weakness
and in much fear and trembling."   I Cor. 2

We comfort others with the same comfort that God gives
us in our affliction.   2 Cor. 1

"I rejoice in my sufferings for your sake, and . . . complete
what is lacking in Christ's afflictions."   Col. 1:24-29

"We have this treasure in earthen vessels, to show that
the transcendent power belongs to God."   2 Cor. 4,6

"I will all the more gladly boast of my weaknesses, that the
power of Christ may rest upon me."   2 Cor. 12

God turns disastrous setbacks into opportunities.   Phil. 1

Vulnerable, like Christ, to hostility and rejection.

                                                   John 15

Necessity is laid upon me.

"Woe to me if I do not preach the gospel! . . . I have become all things to all men, that I might by all means save
some."   1 Cor. 9:15-27

"The divine office which was given to me for you, to make
the word of God fully known."   Col. 1:24-2:6

"To preach . . . the unsearchable riches of Christ . . . the
plan of the mystery hidden for ages in God."   Eph. 3

Accountable to our Master.

"Who then is the faithful and wise steward? . . . Every one
to whom much is given, of him will much be
required."   Luke 12:22-53

The parable of the talents.   Luke 19:11-27

Themes for Prayer

"The fire will test what sort of work each one has
done."   1 Cor. 3:5-23

Death and Hope

*At the heart of the gospel is the belief that in the resurrection
of Jesus God has converted death into the means of transforming
us and bringing us together into fullness of life. We cannot take
this belief to heart unless we face our own fear of death and
through prayer experience again and again the grace to pass
through death to life. In prayer we practice death and open
ourselves to the new life which will finally come to fruition in
heaven.*

Don't be afraid to experience in God's presence our human dread of death.

"You have given me a mere handful of days, and my
lifetime is as nothing in your sight."   Pss. 39, 13, 88, 90

"Let not the torrent of waters wash over me, neither let
the deep swallow me up; do not let the Pit shut its mouth
upon me."   Ps. 69

The anguish of Jesus in the face of death: "Being in agony
he prayed more earnestly; and his sweat became like great
drops of blood falling down upon the ground."
                                            Luke 22:39-46

Part II

"In the days of his flesh, Jesus offered up prayers and supplications, with loud cries and tears, to him who was able to save him from death." Heb. 5:1-10

Jesus grieves over the death of Lazarus. John 11

Jesus' affirmation of life beyond death.
Those who deny the resurrection "know neither the scriptures nor the power of God." Mark 12:18-27

"Your brother will rise again." John 11

"Many will come from east and west and sit at table with Abraham, Isaac, and Jacob in the kingdom of heaven."
Matt. 8:5-13

"Today you will be with me in Paradise." Luke 23:39-43

Jesus is the Resurrection and the Life.
"As the Father raises the dead and gives them life, so also the Son gives life to whom he will." John 5:19-29

"He who eats my flesh and drinks my blood has eternal life, and I will raise him up at the last day." John 6

"I give them eternal life, and they shall never perish, and no one shall snatch them out of my hand. My Father . . . has given them to me." John 10:1-30

"I am the resurrection and the life; he who believes in me, though he die, yet shall he live, and whoever lives and believes in me shall never die." John 11

"He who loves his life loses it, and he who hates his life in this world will keep it for eternal life." John 12:20-36

"In my Father's house are many rooms. . . . I go to prepare a place for you." John 14

"Father, I desire that they also, whom thou hast given me, may be with me where I am." John 17

"Fear not, I am the first and the last, and the living one; I died, and behold I am alive for evermore, and I have the keys of Death and Hades." Rev. 1:4-18

"If we live, we live to the Lord, and if we die, we die to the Lord. . . ." Rom. 14:7-9

"For I am sure that neither death . . . nor anything else in all creation, will be able to separate us from the love of God in Christ Jesus our Lord." Rom. 8

Christ has tasted death for everyone. Heb. 2:5-18

"We were buried therefore with him by baptism into death. . . . If we have been united with him in a death like his, we shall certainly be united with him in a resurrection like his."

Rom. 6:1-11; 2 Tim 2:8-13

For as in Adam all die, so also in Christ shall all be made alive. . . . The last enemy to be destroyed is death. . . . This mortal nature must put on immortality." 1 Cor. 15

In the meantime.

"Though our outer nature is wasting away, our inner nature is being renewed every day. . . . Here indeed we groan, and long to put on our heavenly dwelling." 2 Cor. 4,5

"Now as always Christ will be honored in my body, whether by life or by death. For to me to live is Christ, and to die is gain." Phil. 1:19-26

Part II

212

"Do not be anxious about your life. . . . Which of you by being anxious can add one cubit to his span of life?"

Matt. 6:25-34

The life to come.
"We shall be like him, for we shall see him as he is."

I John 3:1-3

"God will wipe away every tear." Rev. 7:9-17

The wedding banquet. Rev. 19:4-9

God will dwell with them and they shall see his face.

Rev. 21,22

Appendix: The Prayer Stool

This diagram of the prayer stool or seiza bench shows standard dimensions which you can vary slightly to suit your height and build. It is not recommended to have the back of the prayer stool much more than one inch higher than the front and some people prefer a flat, rather than a sloping, seat. Those with carpentry skills can glue the legs into grooves in the underside together with strips of stout molding on both sides, to give support. You can easily make a folding model convenient for travel and storage by using strong hinges to attach the legs to the seat so that they can fold down after use.

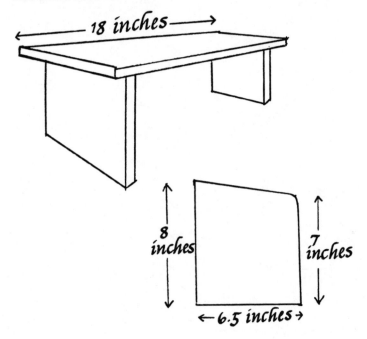